"Mr. George calls things by their right names, faces up to the most difficult and embarrassing situations, records some very sensible advice concerning sex, pornography, alcohol, delinquency, at the same time including much wisdom concerning everyday life with teenagers—in this very helpful book."

—CINCINNATI TELEGRAPH REGISTER

"You may be tired of having psychologists trying to get you to understand your teenage boys, but try this one before giving up the idea. The author writes in the language of teenagers and fathers and mothers."

—MARRIAGE

"Mr. George never bludgeons the reader with his knowledge . . . On the whole, its' a book any parent of teenage boys would want to add to their libraries."

—AVE MARIA

"In these pages of direct talk between counselor and teenager, there is a wealth of helpful insight."

—TOGETHER

"Unusual book—quite different from other guides on this subject—brief but sound advice—nuggets of wisdom—this book presents one problem at a time, examines it, offers suggestions, and then leaves the parents to work it out themselves with their boy. After all, a counselor merely counsels. The parents' job begins where his ends."

—SIGN

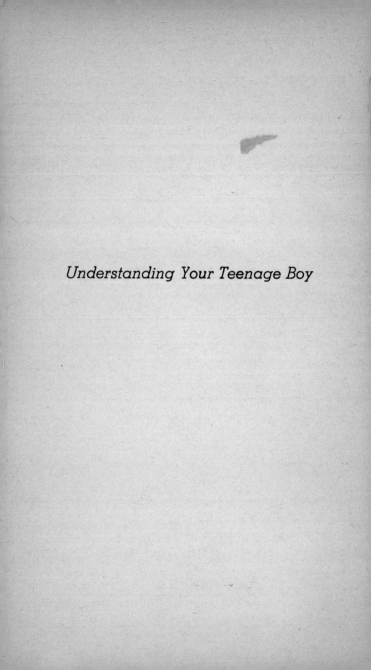

Understanding Your Teenage Boy

Understanding Your Teenage Boy

A PSYCHOLOGIST OPENS HIS CASEBOOK

BY WILLIAM J. GEORGE

ABBEY PRESS
SAINT MEINRAD, INDIANA 47577

© *Sheed and Ward, Inc., 1966*

Library of Congress Catalog Card Number 66-12262

This ABBEY PRESS edition is published by arrangement
with Sheed and Ward, Inc., 1968.

Manufactured in the United States of America.

To Rosemary

CONTENTS

PART THREE—SCHOOL SITUATIONS

PART FOUR—FAMILY SITUATIONS

PART FIVE—SITUATIONS NOT DIS-CUSSED SPECIFICALLY

PART SIX—SUGGESTED READING

INTRODUCTION

Perhaps you are like me. Whenever I pick up a book about a serious subject, I ask, "What training does this author have? Does he know more about the subject than I do?"

To help you decide whether to read this book, therefore, I'll list my reasons why I may know a little more about adolescent boys than you. Here are my reasons:

1. My full-time work is counseling boys between the ages of ten and twenty, as well as their parents, about specific problems. Many specific problems of adolescence are discussed in this book.

2. I genuinely like the boys and parents I counsel. If you and I were to meet, the chances are we would like each other.

3. I have six children of my own: several are adolescents. I view this period of their lives not as a running battle between parents and child but as a planned withdrawal by my wife and myself, with this withdrawal allowing the children to become independent adults.

4. I have obtained all the necessary academic degrees to qualify me for my work. However, this book is not written for the professsional counselor; it is written

for the professional father, YOU. Technical language and Freudian terminology will occur only when laymen's language is vague.

5. I am happily married; I am the master of our household. I think.

1

Home Situations

1. DINNER HOUR

Mix the following ingredients: a mother, a father, six children varying in age from four to eighteen. Place these ingredients at the dining room table over a meat loaf some week-day evening. Add the personalities of the humans—the oldest daughter will want to discuss the currentest events; the oldest son will want to eat hurriedly so he can get to his homework; the next oldest son is the only leisurely liver in the household; the next oldest daughter, if given the opportunity, will interestingly chat throughout the entire meal; the next oldest son will eat his quick fill and then decide it is his turn to describe his day; the youngest daughter, the one with the shrill voice, will talk over, around, and through any conversation; the lovely mother will be concerned with hearing every one and seeing that each eats his share of the food; and the father will occasionally mount his high horse to straighten everybody out and restore a little order.

Result? Mayhem.
The father? Me.

I was the youngest of three boys, and, probably because all I can recall from the dinner conversations of my youth is a continual discussion of how bad business was, my wife and I have always encouraged conversations from the children. You watch a TV program like "The Donna Reed Show" or "My Three Sons" and things run so smoothly, as if by script. You read about the political discussions Joseph P. Kennedy led at his dinner table and you marvel. (Sometimes you wonder, though. How did they keep Teddy from banging his silver cup on the high chair?)

If we had it to do over again, our dinner hour would be better. Here are some of the changes we would make:

We would not insist that a child eat a particular dish served to him. One of my sons didn't touch a potato until he was about eleven, and we battled about this point. As I look up to him to say something today, I believe he is healthy.

We would not correct manners during the dinner hour. My older children have finally learned table manners to the extent that, if we go out for brunch, one will not pick up the grapefruit in his bare hands and squeeze out the juice. Because I hammered the proper-fork-in-the-right-hand routine so hard, my older children have declared open season on the table manners of their younger brothers and sisters.

I would not criticize school efforts or social efforts. Everyone knows that praise should be administered in public and criticism given in private, but *too* often I have made a child lose his eating pleasure.

I would realize that sometimes a child does not want to eat with others: if he wanted to eat the meat loaf alone, he has a reason, and I would respect that reason.

I would not have dinner hour at a specific time each night. I have seen too many foolish arguments develop from my own foolish training that dinner at six is important.

I would respect a child's decision occasionally to eat quietly without participating in the general conversation.

I would be calm at dinner hour. Ha.

One of the questions I usually ask the first time I see a youngster is: "Tell me about your dinner hour last night, will you?"

I've gotten some strange answers.

August 30	I asked the quiet, passive little man, "What do you talk about at the table?" "Hardly nothin'."
November 9	To the same question, "What do you talk about?" another youngster said, "Nothing at all; we watch 'Bat Masterson'."
June 7	"Everything goes fine until the baby spills her milk and then my mother goes up in smoke."
April 6	The little boy gave me the saddest answer.

"What time did you get home last night?"

"About 9," he answered.

"Was that before or after dinner?"

"I don't know." The little boy was ten years old.

Any textbook about the family will tell you that the dinner hour is usually the only time of the day when your entire family gets together, and this hour should be a pleasant training session, with you, the teacher, speaking interestingly and wittingly, guiding the conversation of your charmed captive audience.

Let me know how you make out.

2. COMPARISON WITH OTHERS

Remember the Charlie Chan movies of the late 1930's? In the final scene, after Charlie had thwarted the dastardly schemes of the master criminal, the enemy escaped. The closing line as the camera faded into the fog was, usually, "We must find the insidddddddious Dr. Fu Manchu." And then they found him in the first reel of the next movie, only to lose him once again in the last reel.

"Comparisons with others" are also insidddddddious and almost always present in counseling interviews.

Surely the comparison between an adolescent with routine problems and "the other" makes the adolescent
come out a distant loser. Think for the moment of the
people your son can be compared with—you, your wife,
his older brothers and sisters, his younger brother and
sisters, cousins, neighbor's children, friend's children,
business acquaintance's children—you could fill the
page with names of people who have done better than
your son.

Some parents compare their sons to their brothers.

December 20

Mr. Gebert demonstrated his disapproval of Rick by constantly shak-
ing his head when discussing him.

In answer to my questions about
Rick's progress, Mr. Gebert invar-
iably pointed out how badly Rick
was doing but how well Mike, an
older brother, was doing.

Perhaps my irritation showed
through as I suggested that Mr.
Gebert might be favoring Mike
over Rick. Mr. Gebert agreed with
my thoughts.

As he left the office, Mr. Gebert
reached into a specially reserved
section of his wallet. He said, "Let
me show you Mike's last report
card."

May 31

Mrs. Robinson, quite neurotic, acted as though she wanted to hang
Tom, 16, from a yard arm.

Over and over again she insisted, "My Gary is perfect but that Tom is terrible."

It was "my" Gary and "that" Tom.

March 4   Although the college did not give students E's, Philip, 17, got an E in Latin.

Years before Phil's brother had been an excellent Latin student.

The parents had insisted the young man take Latin; they didn't understand that Phil didn't want to run the Latin race his brother had run so well.

One parent can plant an unfavorable attitude about the other parent in the adolescent's mind too. The youngster, who naturally wants to imitate both parents as adults believes the criticized parent is a failure.

September 3   From the way Mrs. Evans said the words to Jerry, 14, the meaning was clear.

"You're just like your father."

She didn't like her husband.

April 5   I felt sorry for the boy with the child's mind. Evidence indicated he wasn't bright enough to finish high school.

"I've got to finish school this year, Mr George," he pleaded, "'cuz I don't want to be a factory worker like my dad, with his hands cut up and all that all the time."

September 25   I asked, "What job does your father have with the police department, Steve?"
"He's just a patrolman."
Just?

Parents can place their sons in losing competition with themselves, too.

November 14   "I pay my son a dime for every word he finds in the dictionary that I can't define," the intelligent Mr. McIntyre told me.

December 2   I asked him how the dictionary game was going. "Haven't played much lately," he replied. "We've been playing Scrabble."
I wondered who was supposed to be the winner, first at the dictionary game, then at the Scrabble game. I'd bet on the father, myself.

February 1   Tom Farley, 18, said, "No matter which of my friends I bring home, my dad always asks the same question, 'Who's *that* goof?'"

Evidently Mr. Farley thought his own, and Tom's, social position was roughly equivalent to that of a member of the Hindu high caste.

February 10   Mr. Roth was in command of his life but not his son. Jeff was failing high school.

After the army, marriage and four children, Mr. Roth started college. Today, at 45, he is a perpetual student.

Mr. Roth complained, "I get good marks at school—why can't Jeff?"

One of the most vicious comparisons with others is indirect.

November 1   "I'm disappointed with my son."

January 17   "All he ever brings *us* home from school is C's."

Us?

Your disappointment in your son's progress is virtually impossible to conceal from him; but your disappointment may result form unrealistic standards YOU set, standards too high for your son to attain.

With his gauche mannerisms and his awkward hands, your son is not a Xerox copy of you, his older brother, or the lad next door.

Your son is unique.

3. HOBBIES AND READING

One of our family jokes tells about the time my oldest brother and I were playing a golf match against two friends. My brother topped his drive on a tree-lined four par just off the front of the tee, and then I hit a great drive about 270 yards out, leaving me in position for a wedge shot to the green. One of our opponents grumbled, "It's easy to see who was working when you kids grew up!" He was right—my oldest brother drove a tow truck alone when he was nine years old. It is quite easy to look back in our family and analyze what happened; the depression hit when my brother was twenty-one and I ten. He had to work and I was spared the money problems which he faced with our parents. It is possible, though, that he went to work so early that he never developed the capacity to have fun or to have a hobby.

If your parents were like mine, they didn't have time for hobbies, since they had to work long hours and Sundays to keep us in shoes. You and I most probably work less hours than our parents did because of legislation and automation, and as a consequence have the delightful task of teaching ourselves and our sons hobbies without, unfortunately, being able to imitate our own fathers.

What is a hobby? "A favorite pursuit or object," the dictionary tells us, but the dictionary definition falls flat in our context. Let's expand on Webster . . . and the definition becomes "a favorite pursuit or object by a father with his son in order to aid both in the enjoyment of leisure." This definition, a mouthful I'll admit, brings "hobby" to a single point—you and your son select an adventure which will be mutually pleasant. Notice I said "you and your son."

November 19 "What do you and your dad do together for fun—just the two of you?"

      "We go to ball games at Tiger Stadium once in a while."

      "Do you have fun?"

      "He does. He drinks beer all during the game. I don't have any fun."

June 9 "I caddy for my dad when he plays golf."

Again, a little preparation on your part goes a long way.

June 9 Mr. Flach lived for hunting season; he cleaned and oiled his guns weekly.

Jack, 12, went on his first camp-out with his Boy Scout troop.

"The bugs about ate me up," Jack informed me. "I didn't have a mosquito netting."

It was almost as though Mr. Flach wanted to be the outdoor man of the family.

I maintain that the most mutually satisfactory hobby for you and your son is: reading. No matter how sedentary you become, you will be able to pick up the same book he reads.

September 25

My neighbor was walking by our house on his way to the bus, so I gave him a ride downtown.

"Did you start reading *Fate Is The Hunter* that I dropped off for you the other night?" I asked the well-educated man.

"No, not yet, Bill. Every once in a while Danny brings me a book and says, 'Here, Dad, is a book you've GOT to read,' and that's what I'm reading now."

My neighbor showed me the book, a science fiction thriller.

I know Danny well. He's 13.

My neighbor has developed a technique of communicating with his son. No matter what "horrible" escapade Danny has gotten involved in that day, his father can talk about a non-controversial hobby with him —the content matter of Danny's books. And, Danny knows his father appreciates what he is doing.

January 4	I mentioned my neighbor's technique to the mother of one of my clients.

January 24	"How's the reading program coming along?" I asked the same lady.
	    "Not too good. I just can't get my son interested."
	    "What have you been reading?"
	    "The Bible, every night."

So, if your son develops an interest in money, marbles, or a tubful of turtles, your best bet is to get interested in the same hobby. By making books at his reading level handy to him, you can start him reading; by reading those same books with him he will know you like him. His hobby of the day will mature with age, but in the meantime you will have established a superb channel for conversation.

4. ALLOWANCES AND HOUSEHOLD DUTIES

If you were to sail in the front door of your home tonight with a box of candy under your arm for your wife, I think you could have one or two reasons in mind: either you would think of the candy as a bargaining tool to assist you in some past or future negotiations with her, or you would be offering the candy as a gift in appreciation of her loveliness. Some parents see an allowance as a gift to their children, judging from the frequently asked question, "How much should I give my son for an allowance?" The question gives me the opportunity to say I believe an allowance is not a gift, and in addition that there are two types of allowance, the home allowance and the school allowance. Let me show you what I mean.

First, the home allowance. When a boy is about twelve years old the great American pastime is to toss him the following grenade:

> Parent: "Well, son, it's time you learned a little responsibility around the house. Starting tomorrow we want you to burn the papers every day, clean out the garage every Saturday, and . . ."

If his answer were, "Sure Dad," he would be an extraordinarily respectful child. More probably, since he is going to be doing more physical labor tomorrow than he did today, his answer would be, "Who, me?"

His answer is not as disrespectful as you might think. Suppose your boss approached you tomorrow at work and said, "Management has decided we can get along without Mr. Jackson over there. Starting tomorrow morning, you do your own job and his, too."

You would scream like a banshee and begin instantly to renegotiate your contract; your son would renegotiate with you if he had your bargaining experience.

How much a week is it worth to you to have an incompetent but interested young man clean out the incinerator weekly, burn the papers daily, dust and vacuum the first floor once a week, and perform whatever other household tasks you and he agree upon? You might come up with a package deal. (You have one advantage . . . he doesn't know the value of a buck the way you do and you may be able to hire him for less than the union scale.) Then, if he blows one of his chores, you are in the driver's seat when you say, "Son, you didn't clean your room well enough this week. I think we'd better chop your allowance by a quarter this week, but try harder next week, will you?" He can't argue because he knows he was hasty cleaning his room.

Please don't misinterpret my remarks. When I ask one of my children to run an errand, I'm not about to bargain with him about how much money I will pay him for the time involved. In such an instance I try to have in mind some unselfish act I have done for that child recently, so if he gives me the "Who, me?" treatment, I can then remind him that others take care of his personal requirements, too. In this section of the chapter I am stressing the routine chores you may ask your son to perform.

The other type of allowance is the school allowance. Think for a moment of the commitments contained in the following short conversation:

> *Father:* "How much allowance will you need this year at school?"
>
> *Son:* "Well, bus fare is fifty cents a day, and I want to buy milk and dessert each day at school. I should have $1.00 a week for recreation, and a quarter for the church collection. How about $5.00 a week?"
>
> *Father:* " Sounds a little high to me, but I guess it's ok."

The son has agreed to perform . . . he will go to school regularly, will spend $1.00 a week for recreation, and attend church regularly. The father has agreed to perform, too, by paying his son for services rendered. If the father does not pay his son regularly, in the son's mind the father is a cheat.

I've seen parents who seem to relish their ability to attack their sons in the wallet; in a later chapter we will discuss at some length the father who would agree to a weekly allowance for his children and then, at pay-off time, develop reason after reason why the children should be underpaid. The laborer is worthy of his hire.

"How much money should my son get a week?"

It depends. It depends, primarily of course, on how much money you are able to donate to the cause. I remember the wealthiest kid in my own high school class and how poorly he turned out, and I remember the poorest kid in the class, and how well accepted he was by his friends. Even if you can afford it, your son should not have more money than his friends; if you cannot afford it, don't worry about it.

Summarizing what we've said, one type of allowance is payment to your son for performing household chores regularly and the other type furnishes your son with necessary school and recreation spending money. If you mix the two types, and, for example, cut off his home allowance but continue to insist he clean closets although he gets poor marks in school, in his mind you are unfair.

Any allowance agreement you reach with your son differs from the standard labor contract in one important aspect—the length of the contract. When a labor leader sits down at, or perhaps stands on, a bargaining desk, the final contract guarantees performance for a specific length of time. Your son's life, however, changes almost daily, and he might, for example, change his class schedule so he would not need lunch money; your life, too, might change rapidly because of illness or work stoppages. It might be wise to leave your contract with your son open-ended in the sense that either of you can immediately renegotiate if circumstances change.

Here's what you can gain in your family from the proper use of allowance money:

Your son will learn the importance of abiding by the terms of a contract.

By his performance, your son will increase his sense of personal achievement.

As he observes the businesslike manner in which you handle the contract, his respect and admiration for you will grow.

5. COMPULSIONS

From the cocktail party definition of the word "compulsion," everyone is compulsive. You are compulsive about being to work on time, your wife is compulsive about doing the dishes after supper, your son is compulsive about combing his hair, your dog is compulsive about walking in circles before lying down. You hear the comment, "there's nothing wrong about being compulsive—that's what makes railroads run on time." The word is misused sometimes because the user does not understand the complete definition—a compulsion is the tendency to repeat over and over a certain kind of behavior DESPITE ITS INAPPROPRIATENESS.

Compulsions, in my book, take a long time to build and as a consequence do not occur frequently in the adolescent. However, the young man who showers twice an evening, peeps into neighbors' bedroom windows, or refuses to step on a sidewalk crack is crying loudly for help; if you see your son repeating some inappropriate activity frequently, by all means take him to your family physician.

The backlash of living with a compulsive parent can cause lifelong complication to a youngster: the youngster lives in the surly house he knows, absorbs the inappropriate activities of the compulsive parent(s), and then adds his own quirks to the inappropriate activities later in his life.

What will happen to Mike?

June 28	Mike McGlynn, 12, was failing summer school. If he continued failing, he would repeat the seventh grade the second time. He would sometimes bang his head on the bedroom wall, it was reported.
July 11	Mrs. McGlynn called to say she had a headache and could not bring Mike in; his father would bring him. Mr. McGlynn bragged about Mike doing the dishes well and changing the new baby expertly.
July 31	Mrs. McGlynn could not come in. Mike, here alone, talked about his

mother "getting headaches from us kids," making the beds herself "in a special way" every day.

August 5 Mrs. McGlynn could not come in. Mike declared that his mother had "spring cleaning every Friday," insisted her husband bathe the children every night while she nursed "the headache."

I never did see the elusive Mrs. McGlynn; she was too busy forcing everyone in the house to conform inexorably to her inappropriate actions.

Mike? He'll be an excellent housekeeper some day. Unless the unlikely occurs and his father starts to manage the household.

A compulsive parent needs rules like water needs a glass . . . if you take the glass away, the water spills all over the sink.

Summer Mr. Gorman paints his house on the outside without assistance from anyone. He has no trouble chipping paint off the woodwork because, you see, he paints the outside of his house every summer.

Mr. Gorman is 74 years old.

Home Situations

October 9   Most lights in the Stein's house
could not be turned on. If any of
the nine children turned a forbidden switch, Mr. Stein would remove the bulb from the socket.

When the streetlights went on,
so did the kitchen light bulb;
everyone gathered in the kitchen
to read and to study.
Mr. Stein was a superior ma-
chinist with a paycheck to match
his abilities.

What is a parent trying to accomplish with a compulsion? The bride who insists that her guests remove
their shoes at the front door is not (as she thinks), concerned with keeping the new rug clean: she is trying
to show herself she is strong enough to make others
obey her.

I've never met a person completely uncompulsive.
Can compulsive people be categorized? I think so.
Let's look at compulsions with an "uproar" microscope;
if your compulsions are your own little blankets and
cause no uproar in your family or yourself, you'll be
happier if you keep them.

I know where I got one of my compulsions, the one
about being on time. My mother used to sit on the
steaming living room radiator with her hat and coat on,
ready ten minutes before departure time. When our
older children were young, I used to be one of those
dinner-at-six people, but I noticed the unneccessary uproar I caused my long-suffering wife and no longer insist on that inappropriate behavior. Now we're work-

32

ing on the older children to help them be less demanding that dinner be ready at six.

We're having lots of uproar, too.

6. STEALING

Autumn

My lovely wife sat next to me on the couch after our children had gone to bed.

"Mary stole a package of gum at the supermarket today when I wasn't looking. She stuffed all the gum into her mouth after we got home, and that's how I happened to notice her. What's the explanation for that, psychologist?"

The way she said "psychologist" made me consider my answer carefully.

I finally commented, "The child who steals feels he is unloved."

"What? You love her and I love her—everybody loves a four-year-old. How can you say that?"

"Notice what I said, dear. I wasn't denying our love for Mary; I simply said she *feels* unloved."

You will notice that often statements are vague throughout this book, vague through my use of qualifying words like "probably" "usually," and "perhaps." When I don't know all the circumstances surrounding a youngster's problem, I can't be exact. But here is one time I will be exact—the child who steals feels unloved. I'll even include this instance:

October 13   Al, 14, had a long list of police offenses, ranging from stealing a jacket to breaking into a neighbor's home.

Al's father passed handbills door-to-door when he worked, and lived common-law with a second wife. Al's mother had given up any resistance and escaped into the bottle.

Utilities had been turned off in the hovel where Al lived.

Legally, Al was a thief, but he had no jacket and no food. If I were a lawyer I could defend him; Al, at 14, was wistfully searching for someone to love him.

December 4   Reggie Hardy, 17, was suspended from high school for stealing fifty-one textbooks. He didn't take the books in order to study them, I'm sure, nor did he need money.

Mr. Hardy was the hard-work type one can come to dislike in my profession. He worked ten hours a day six days a week until he had a heart attack and then resumed the same schedule after recuperating.

Reggie to his father was someone who stayed at the house and would continue to stay there until he moved on.

January 10

Bob Michaels went Christmas shopping. With money in his pocket and his younger brother as a witness, he walked out of the discount store without passing the cashier.

The younger brother spread the word.

Mr. Michaels had a pattern of promising gifts and entertainment for his sons and then backing away. Several times he would agree to weekend camping trips and then never leave the post.

November 9

Larry Ptak, 13, was under-achieving at school. I visited the home because no one there could take the time to bring him into the office.

The Ptak family included at least a dozen children. I arrived about 4 p.m., just in time to watch Mrs. Ptak feed her shift of children cafeteria style before leaving for work. Mr. Ptak was due home at 5 p.m. to be the night babysitter.

The whole house was being run by an eleven-year-old girl who had learned her shouting from an expert.

December 2 It was during this interview, I think, that I first heard about the movie camera, but I heard about it so indirectly I missed the point.

December 16 By now it was common knowledge that Larry had stolen an expensive camera from a truck parked outside a department store.

I suggested to Larry and his mother, "Take it back."

January 3 On another house call, I saw the camera in its place of honor on the living room mantel.

I said, "Take it back."

January 17 Mrs. Ptak wasn't home, so the eleven-year-old housekeeper handed me the camera while the other children commented about Larry's crime.

I dropped the camera off at the department store on the way home.

Was Larry stealing or substituting—stealing a $200 camera or substituting for the affection they worked so hard to avoid giving him?

March 4   Ralph, 14, was legally adopted by loving parents. He liked their home much better than the orphanage and settled down well until about six weeks ago when his natural mother saw him in a supermarket. She entered his life for the first time.

April 16   Ralph was suspended from school for stealing seventy-five cents.

Whom did he love?

Sometimes it seems P. T. Barnum is still a basic hero to Americans. We read with delight how the Brinks robbery was meticulously planned and executed . . . we chuckle at the lady who, without legal signatures, distributed over a million dollars from a savings and loan association to her friends. But, let this striving youngster of ours be hustled home some night for lifting a package of cigarettes and you'd think it was another

Teapot Dome scandal. It would be better to accept the fact that he stole the cigarettes and then investigate thoroughly your own relationship with him. I'll bet he isn't trying to steal cigarettes; he is trying to steal your heart away from its disinterest in him.

7. VACATIONS

A vacation is a wonderful time—time to rest and recharge for the grueling fifty weeks ahead. Yet, when you have an adolescent son around, it may be wise to consider what he wants in a vacation, so your vacation is not harassed with displeasure. A trip to Gettysburg may be ideal for the eight-year-old who will see Confederate soldiers behind every rock along the Chambersburg Pike, but boring for the fifteen-year-old who stands where Warren stood on Little Round Top and then dismays his parents with the question, "What's next?"

The adolescent is primarily interested in being with groups his own age; he has naturally lost an interest in being with his family for long periods because he feels he has learned everything he can from associations with that family. So, if you drop your son into a situation where these associations are constant, he will probably raise enough havoc or at least exhibit enough boredom to damage your own vacation.

August 4

"The summer home belongs to my mother-in-law, Mr. George. Both she and my husband believe it's my job to open the place up every spring, stay there all summer with the kids, entertain everyone she invites, and then close it for the winter. I'd much rather stay home."

August 18

Expansively, the dominating man described the same summer home without mentioning that his mother owned it.

I finally broke in to ask, "How does your wife like it up there?"

"She loves it."

July 9

"Yeah, we went to the cottage again last weekend, Mr. George," Rudy Marshall, 16, grunted.

"Have any fun?"

"Nope. This time my twelve-year-old cousin was there. My mother wouldn't talk to me for two days after I told her I wasn't going to baby-sit for no girl."

Mr. Marshall was popping mad at Rudy's lack of co-operation. I tried to convey, without success, the thought that the Marshalls could just have well stayed home for all the pleasure any of them

had had. Mr. Marshall believed
that everybody automatically loved
cottage life.

The lady who wrote, "Vacations—my husband fishes
all day long," was saying that while he sat in the boat,
she sat.

The father who discovers he only has five hundred
miles to drive the last day out on a trip and heads down
the super highway toward the barn is not going to be
rested.

Some parents seem to glory in the fact they are so
devoted to their families they do not have time for vacations. I'm sorry for these people:

"Vacations- haven't been taking any."
"Vacations- rarely."
"Vacations- don't take any."
"Vacations- stay home, catch up on work."
"Vacations- haven't had one yet."
"Vacations- don't interest me."
"Vacations- none."
"Vacations- four years since the last one."

Is it possible that these parents had such horrible
times on their vacations when they were children themselves that they refuse to believe that vacations can be
a ball for everyone?

Advantages are there for both you and your children
if you can take your wife for an occasional weekend.
Time with your wife will make you realize you both

have the same goals, even if you do seem to have different daily directions, and at the same time, your children will realize how important you both are to them when you are at home.

If you as a parent have the summer camp pattern—as soon as school finishes the children leave for camp for the entire summer—I doubt whether you would read this book.

In summary, the age of your son should be a factor which makes you take a close look at where you vacation. If you have been visiting the same place every summer for years, you may well find that several members of the family would prefer to change the routine.

"Vacations are for families," another client wrote. I agree, to the extent that the larger the family, the more planning you and your wife should make to insure the pleasure of all.

8. GRANDPARENTS

Visualize the old time country school, pot-bellied stove and all. There are just a few students of different ages in the class; the teacher is young and dedicated. One day an older teacher walks into the school room, an older teacher in retirement with time on her hands, ready to hand down all she knows about teaching children. An ideal teaching situation?

Not necessarily.

Sometimes the older teacher forgets she is sidelined and tries to run the entire class, young teacher and all.

April 30

The Hoffman family wanted placement for Jimmy, 11, because he had run away from home several times. Each time he was found at his grandfather's house.

Lines of financial strain showed on Mr. Hoffman's face. His wife had been hospitalized for five months recently; transfusions and round-the-clock nurses had pushed the family deep into a monetary hole. Mrs. Hoffman went back to work as a secretary.

May 2

Jim, according to his father, had not run away until after his mother returned from the hospital. While she was hospitalized, Jim ate his lunch at his grandfather's and stayed there weekends.

May 5

Mrs. Leonard, Jim's school counselor, called to assert, irately, that the boy had gone to his grandfather's house that day instead of to school. She was "of good mind to go over and haul Jimmy out of bed" at noon. I encouraged the action.

May 15

By this time, it was obvious what Jimmy wanted—the attention and affection of his grandfather.

And, it was obvious what the grandfather wanted—the affection and attention of his grandson. He was going to show Jimmy's parents the proper way to raise a boy, no matter what they wanted.

And, sometimes the older teacher does not agree with the teaching methods of the younger teacher.

July 27

Mr. Nelson's father evidently didn't think much of the way his son was raising Paul, 14. The grandfather made sure he saw Paul every week-end, mostly to criticize the way the boy's step-mother was raising him.

Paul then would come home and provoke vicious fights with his brother and with students at school.

August 10

Paul was so listless he could hardly talk. He was sunburned badly; his grandfather had taken him to a nearby lake for an outing and had gotten drunk while Paul was burning.

Mrs. Nelson commented she couldn't understand why 'grand-pop' didn't remember that people sunburn.

I understood, I thought; the grandfather was causing as much commotion as he could to the marriage.

Sometimes the older teacher refuses to give the authority of making decisions to the younger teacher.

November 13   "Who would you say is the boss of your family when your dad isn't home?" I asked the bright youngster.

"Oh, grandma is. She's the boss when my dad's home, too"!

Sometimes, also, the older teacher is incompetent to begin with.

January 5   Mark's grandfather must have been something. Vicious with a bull whip, he had driven all of his seven children out of his house in their early teens.

March 6   The man my age said, "My father worked on the railroad, Mr. George. The only time he came home was to change his clothes, and he always had another woman besides my mother."

August 14

"You take care of raising the boys until they are fourteen," the man told his wife years ago. "Then, I'll take over."

Then he would leave home after dinner to seek love and consolation from his own mother.

By the time the boys were fourteen, their patterns of conformity were established, but the patterns they established didn't conform with morality.

February 12

"My mother has always blamed me for breaking up her marriage to my dad," the lady said.

I asked her, "How old were you when your parents were divorced?"

"Nine."

Grandparents sometimes change their methods. Your father, if he now realizes he raised you too strictly, may over-adjust his past errors by being too lenient with your son. If you as a child didn't have much money, your father may try to make himself feel better about his earlier financial setbacks by buying his way into your son's heart.

We parents must evaluate as objectively as we can just how well our own parents raised us. So, let's take a long hard look at the older teacher. If you like the way you were raised, by all means consult your own parents for guidance in handling specific adolescent problems. If your parents were incompetent with you they will probably be incompetent still.

And, by all means, set the stage so your parents only give advice when you specifically ask for it.

The younger teacher, after all, lives more intimately with the pupils and knows modern living problems better.

For my money, I'll bet on the younger teacher any day.

9. ODD BEHAVIOR

In later chapters, particulary those about "Clothing," "Companions," "Dating," and "Verbal Hostility," the underlying theme will be that the typical adolescent, in his need to become a mature person, often turns away from parents' influences to associate with groups which have the same temporary goals he does. In this chapter our attention turns to the youngster who causes concern to his parents because he does not conform to society's standards and who is *not* primarily a member of a group performing the same non-conforming activities. The adolescent who is a brilliant student but who engages in no extra-curricular activities, the girl who practices piano five hours a day seven days a week, the boy who draws superb cartoons of his classmates and teachers during class, the young man who puts his shirt on backwards, are not acting like most teen-agers.

The first question to ask is, "Who says the adolescent is acting oddly?"

Unfortunately, many times the parents alone maintain that the adolescent's behavior is peculiar.

October 22 Bill Green, 18, was a car thief. On the positive side of the ledger, his marks were practically all A's in a difficult trade school.

His mother had refused to allow him, when he was sixteen, to take the usual driver training course because he was "too young."

Bill now wanted to buy a junk automobile and pay for its repair out of his earnings from a drug store job. He was "too young."

He read automotive and electronics magazines voraciously. His mother's opinion was that these magazines were like dirty pictures.

Here was a rare eighteen-year-old young man—rare because he had some idea of what he wanted to do in life—work in mechanical activities.

And his mother? She was erecting road blocks for Bill.

We parents have weaknesses of our own, weaknesses which we find difficult to perceive, and when we spot one of our weaknesses popping out in our son, we hammer hard.

October 30	Carl Snite, 10, curly haired and vocal, came in because he was not socializing enough.
	I've talked to quiet young men and I couldn't see where Carl fitted the pattern. He was on the honor roll at school, rode a bike with his friends, was building a fort near his home.
	Mrs. Snite emphasized how Carl would come home from school and sit "for hours" looking out the window.
November 14	Mrs. Snite declared that Carl was still sitting by the window, not volunteering in class.
	Carl maintained that he had been flying kites with his friends, and visiting the nearby dairy bar with them.
	I asked Carl to keep a diary for me—a diary of his more important daily activities, until I saw him again. He agreed readily.
November 27	Carl handed me his diary with the comment, "I averaged volunteering

4½ times a day in class." The diary affirmed that he had played with his friends almost every day.

Confronted with the written evidence, Mrs. Snite admitted that Carl socialized better, but still "not enough." Then she revealed that she herself had never been able to socialize well. Her mother, who lived with the family, still ordered her around.

Carl, then, seemed to be in this position. He could never socialize enough to satisfy his mother's need for socialization.

November 9

There is a parochial high school in Detroit which admits about 200 freshmen each September out of about 1500 applicants.

Mike, 16, just barely made the scholastic entrance requirements two years ago; since then he had been barely passing or barely failing his courses.

He played saxophone well enough in a small combo to earn his tuition and keep himself in clothing.

Mike wanted to drop out of the school and attend a public school which would be easier and yet had a statewide reputation for its band.

Mike's father said "No." He would continue at the parochial school.

There is probably not a parent among us who would not be delighted with his seventeen-year-old son if the son were to say, "I've decided what I want to do in life, Dad. I want to be a . . ." We would run out and arrange a second mortgage on our homes to help in his career. I frequently ask young men I counsel, "What do you want to do in life?" and am never surprised by the shrugged-shoulder answer. I am not surprised because I know I am asking a young man to make a decision about which he knows very little—he can't decide about studying to become a CPA because he doesn't know what a CPA does. So, if your son exhibits what you decide is odd behavior, it might be well to see if his behavior is objectively odd or odd because he is not conforming with what you want him to do.

Perhaps because I am one to decide what I want to do in life, I've smiled at this thought:
If a man does not keep pace with his companions, perhaps it is because he hears a different drummer. Let him step to the music which he hears, however measured or far away.

Thoreau was a bit of an oddball, too.

10. VERBAL HOSTILITY

Hostility is there in my office all day long—the child despises his head-shrinker, resents his father falling asleep nightly in front of the TV set, accuses his mother of picking on him every time she sees him—the mother believes I am taking only her son's side, states he never cleans up his closet, knows her husband is not a good father and mate—the father is sure he can run his family without outside assistance, maintains his son won't obey him, thinks his wife is sexually cold. I often feel hostility fuming up around me like smoke. But if I were to react to the verbal hostility shown me and become hostile myself, my interviews would be short, explosive, and infrequent. A vital part of my work is to help parents understand why children become extremely hostile in adolescence.

July 6   "My son told me he wasn't going to cut the damn grass."

We parents can often allow a typical statement like this teen-ager's to trigger explosions which reverberate for days. We lump all the natural demonstrations of hostility into one category and know the boy is on his way to incorrigibility.

Something positive, miserable to live with but still positive, is happening when a child starts arguing with his parents. He is leaving the ways of the child in which he was taught automatically to obey your orders and entering the ways of the adult. As you must be convinced before you act, so must he. Again he is trying to imitate you.

September 12   Denny Rady, 16, and his father
rushed in. He had run away from
school and home, and had been
arrested for truancy.

Mr. Rady, mean and noble, was
the instant obedience type. If he
wanted the basement steps swept at
midnight, Denny, damn it, would
sweep the basement steps.

"Do you ever let Denny make
up his own schedule for household
duties and then check it with
him?" I asked.

It was a brand new thought for
Mr. Rady; yet Denny's model for
manhood was an independent
man.

The more independent you are as a father and busi-
nessman, the more verbal hostility your son will show.
If you were dominated by your wife, a Milquetoast, you
probably wouldn't be reading this chapter because your
son would not display much language hostility. And
so, a lot of the verbal battles your boy starts are not
evidences of hostility against YOU, but hostility against
being treated as a child. A psychiatrist recently told me
about his own four adolescent children, "They're driving me crazy."

Like a mathematical formula: Adolescent's hostility
+ your understanding = diminished hostility.

Assume you are sitting across the desk from me: you
are fed up with all of my stupid suggestions and de-

clare nastily, "We've been coming to see you for four months now and our son is worse than when we started. I see no point in coming back."

I counter-punch your verbal hostility with some of my own. "That's fine with me. I've been trying to convey the thought every time I see you that the biggest problem in your house is you. Besides, I'm busy." What have we got?

Hostility $+$ hostility $=$ animosity.

And, which came first, your hostility or mine?

If you're running into a lot of lip from your son, maybe it's time for you to stop telling him what to do and calmly convince him to act like an adult.

11. CONSISTENCY OF DISCIPLINE

I've run into some parents who are consistent in disciplining their children.

July 7

"We seem to have more trouble at the dinner table than any other time, Mr. George," Mrs. O'Reilly stated. "My husband insists that if Bob asks for a second helping of meat, he must also eat a second helping of every other course."

Bob was 13, five feet tall, weighed 130 pounds—one of those boys it is easier to step over than walk around.

August 9

Joe, 17, was smiling as he made the remark, "I've been grounded so many times I feel like a lifer," but the remark was serious.

March 2

"As soon as I walk in the front door after leaving the station, my wife tells me all the troubles Don has had that day. I have to spank him practically before I say hello every night."

January 4

"My dad gets mad at somebody in the family and stays mad at everybody."

December 9

After Morry, 14, stole his first car, his father quashed all police charges against him.

The second offense was more serious—he cracked up another stolen automobile to the tune of $600 worth of damages.

Mr. Delmar, like a proprietary master of ceremonies, explained,

"The insurance company is not going to press charges: the owner of the car has his own insurance to cover the damages."

"What about Morry?" I asked.

"I think he's learned his lesson," his father said.

And I've seen some situations I would judge show inconsistency of discipline.

August 4   I was thumbing through my police referrals about Eddie as I asked the question, "What did your father do after you stole those two cars?"

Eddie's voice cracked to a falsetto. "First time, he beat me good with a belt buckle. The second time, he took me to a Coney Island hot dog stand and asked me why I done it."

May 6   The young man told me that his father had forbidden him to talk on the phone to girls while he was grounded.

"Mom lets me call 'em, though, while Dad's at work."

October 30   "That's what bugs me—my parents. They're mean sometimes, sometimes MEAN."

I've seen some cases of no discipline, too, like the fifteen-year-old whose father bought him his own car before he was legally able to drive, the mother who drank up the Welfare checks instead of supplying food and lodging for her son, the fourteen-year-old who had acquired a step-father and then wasn't allowed to come home before 10 p.m. each night.

"Discipline" can be defined as "training that strengthens"; the same dictionary says "consistency" is "without self-contradiction." To the definitions let me add the phrase "without parental pop-off," meaning "calmly, without haste." If you and he agreed yesterday that he should be home at 10 p.m., the agreement might have been valid then but he may come in tonight at 10:30. Please, Dad, no pop-off. Your son has changed from yesterday because he is trying to establish rules HE can live by.

At his age, I'll guarantee one thing about your son. If you order him to obey you or punish him without listening to his side of the discussion, you will get an argument. If you take the time to explain why you are establishing rules, he will be able to clarify in his own mind what your restrictions are, and thereby avoid infractions. If situations develop for which you have not agreed upon regulations with your son, you as a father can only resort to the lame statement, "You should have known better."

Who should be the main discussants in the discipline debate? Your boy has a man, you, whom he wants to emulate and understand, and if you hand down your *dicta* through your wife or don't hand down those *dicta* at all, he will not absorb your viewpoints.

All too frequently I have seen fathers abdicate their discipline rights, problems, and duties, to others. Most often it is the wife who wields the heavy stick or yields it, but sometimes it is someone else.

July 10 "My husband and I agree on how Jerry should behave, Mr. George, but then grand-pop puts his two cents in."

December 13 "My older sister, she's married, comes over almost every day and tells me what a disappointment I am to my parents."

"My oldest brother is always beating me up for not cleaning up my room."

This is the first time you and I have been parents. So, we may shy away from discussing with our sons what discipline means to their futures. When you think back of close order drill in the service, yearly visits to the dentist, arriving at work on time, you and I have learned that discipline is training that strengthens. We can help our sons learn that discipline is beneficial to the man.

2

Social Situations

12. COMPANIONS

In the early 1900's a man named Cooley developed a theory about society which has stood up under sociologists' barrages ever since. He maintained that every individual is a member of "primary" and secondary" groups. A "primary" group is closely knit with common goals and affection between individuals—your family unit is a primary group. As the child grows to school age, he starts associating with other toddlers. In school and in the neighborhood, he starts "joining secondary groups." There is really no sharp distinction between the primary and secondary groups, just a gradual leaving of the nest. We join a secondary group to gain something from that group. A secondary group may be as closely knit as your weekly poker group or as loosely knit as a crowd at a football game.

Think back over the last few years of all of the social activities your son has started—and promptly dropped. He may have worn a maroon sweat shirt because "everybody is wearing them," or called everyone with whom he does not sympathize a "fink," or stuck a comb in his right hip pocket. He is being influenced by his secondary groups and he wants to be accepted by these groups. One encouraging point is that when he makes up his mind that his goals surpass the group aims, he will change groups. (He may even have his hair cut!)

We can visualize primary and secondary group relationships by placing them on opposite ends of a teeter-totter. If your family relationship is weak for any one of a number of reasons, your son will be much more interested in acceptance by far-out groups.

May 15 — Anthony O'Konsky, 16, wore his hair long; his pointed shoes were worn from so much standing around street corners. He had been skipping school and associating with bad companions.

Mr. O'Konsky treated the visit here as a short cut to Tony's improvement. The father and mother had been in German prison camps for years. Mr. O'Konsky did not finish grade school.

When I suggested that the parents could start speaking English at home and in general become more American, a curtain dropped over Mr. O'Konsky's eyes.

There was nothing to be corrected at home—the trouble was with Tony.

May 29 — The O'Konskys failed to keep an appointment. I called the house but they were not interested in coming back.

> I think I'll be reading Tony's name in the paper one of these days; he is not a difficult boy to pray for.

The O'Konskys may have had a strong family when viewed from old country standards but in Tony's adolescent judgment, his parents did not stack up. He escaped into drinking with his hoody crowd.

By reversing the teeter-totter, the family group can become so strong that the child is fearful of joining secondary groups . . . he feels that nobody can approach the specifications set by his parents.

August 2

> Mrs. Sondheim brought home a larger weekly pay check than her husband. She wore a sharp dagger of deprecation for Jack, 17, and yet Jack was an all A student in an electronics course. He also worked six full days a week in a discount drug store.
>
> Mrs. Sondheim had found some lewd magazines in Jack's dresser.
>
> Jack seemed to be searching almost wistfully for someone to soften his mother. "She bawls me out fifty times a day," he said.
>
> Jack did not date: he simply retired from combat to his room to study.

With Mrs. Sondheim's pattern of protesting it was easy to guess what would have happened if Jack had brought friends home. They could not possibly have satisfied this lady who kept her home atmosphere like a Finnish sauna.

It is time to place the teeter-totter in the middle position where it should be. If you encourage your son to join secondary groups and then help him screen his friends, you should be able to help him. You have the calm right to meet his friends in *your* living room and he has the calm duty of arranging the meeting on your home grounds.

Be kind to your son's friends, if you will. He is seeking sympathetic acceptance from his friends, but more importantly he is seeking your acceptance of him and his friends because you are his model for manhood. If you like them, he feels again that you like what he is doing.

13. CLOTHES

Patio living, with or without a patio, has affected us men, and I for one am delighted with the informal clothes we can wear. A generation ago my father would not have entertained friends without wearing a suitcoat but when my wife and I played bridge the other night, I wore a sport shirt, a Christmas sweater, and slacks, and so did our host. After all, women's clothes styles change almost monthly, judging from the depart-

ment store charge account slips we pay every month
and so why shouldn't men's clothes styles become more
comfortable, less formal? (I keep waiting for the day
when the white shirt is not the badge of the executive.
Will it ever come?)

Strangely, one of the biggest pitched battles I arbi-
trate is between father and adolescent son over the
question of what is legitimate apparel and what is not.

I see three main types of clothing worn by teen-agers,
each of which gives an insight into the boy's CUR-
RENT thinking:

1. The boy who imitates his father's apparel.
2. The "frat," characterized by a short brush hair
cut, a tie only when neccessary, and light colored
clothes.
3. The "grease," who has an extremely long hair-do,
dark clothes, black boots, and, this week, a comb with
a handle sticking out of his right hip pocket.

Parents seldom criticize the clothes worn by the first
two types but I pity the poor "grease." (If I were to
call you a grease or you were to call me one, we might
come to blows, but the teen-aged grease likes to be
called a grease; it is a badge of belonging for him.)

August 24   Mr. Morgan was one of those men
determined to make the ball
bounce in his direction. Randy, a
grease, had been grievously de-
linquent for insisting on wearing
a pair of "points," black pointed-
toed boots.

"I'm a native Detroiter," I said,
"and I can remember when I was

about Randy's age our group used to wear key chains from our belt loop down to the knee and back up to our right hand pockets."

"I used to wear one of those, too," he gasped, "and I had a marble on the end of it. Did you have a marble in your pocket?"

"No, not even any keys."

I waited for the understanding. No laugh.

I finally leaned around the corner of my desk, stared at his trouser leg, and asked, "Are you still wearing that key chain?"

The clothes your son wears are his keys of admission to groups he wants to join. If a particular group wears pink button-down sweaters and he finds out that he has the same goals as they do, the chances are he will be bugging you for a pink sweater. And when he exhausts his needs for that pink sweater group, he will join another group.

September 2   "Your hair is a lot shorter, George. You're not turning into a frat on me, are you?" I asked.

Sheepishly, very sheepishly, George said, "Aw, I joined the school wrestling team and it would be suicide to wrestle with long hair."

George had exhausted his need for belonging to his "grease group" and moved into a group which had a need for wrestling.

One of the saddest youngsters I have seen was one who was a complete grease except for his hair, which his mother had cut completely off. He was as bald as a basketball. In about twenty years some old friend of his will say, "Say, Mike, remember the time your mother shaved your head?" and Mike will shake his head at the lack of understanding she showed to him.

Why impose our adult clothes standards on our youngsters? Your boy's clothing will mature as he does, and besides, maybe the non-tie generation we are raising will emancipate us old men from our cravat shackles.

14. DRIVING

(You may question my discussion of driving as a "Social Situation" rather than a "School" or "Home" one. I have reasons . . . and I ask that if you read this chapter you also read the next chapter on "Car Theft." The chapters interlock.)

When I was a boy (ahem) things were different. Your family either had the money to own an automobile or it didn't; learning to drive occurred on country roads with a number of dented fenders in traffic later on, but I can't recall that driving a car was so important to the teen-ager then as it is now. Take TV commercials today—have you ever seen one of a teen-ager *walking* beside a Chevy Corvette? Everybody drives, and the need to drive is important to your boy. Note that I am merely talking about one NEED, the driving NEED, and not the driving NEED in connection with his NEED to do homework or his NEED to pick up his shoes under the dining room table.

I've seen too many parents confuse needs.

(In Michigan, fifteen-year-olds can take driver training at authorized locations. If a boy passes, he can obtain his driver's license on his sixteenth birthday.)

April 23

Tom King was a tall slim sixteen-year-old with a smiling personality. He was so tense his fingers were bitten raw.

After much argument, Mr. King had agreed to let Tom take driver training on two conditions: 1) Tom had to improve his C average to a B, and 2) Tom had to maintain the car by working part time in a drug store.

Tom had *never* had higher than a C average: he lost the use of the car the night his next report card arrived.

Mr. King's main weapon against Tom was restricting the use of the car. If Tom left his room untidy or came to the table with a dirty face, away went driving privileges.

May 10

Tom struggled his marks up to B's but received a traffic ticket for tailgating. Away went driving privileges and away went Tom—to Missouri in a stolen car.

His father brought him back and let him drive with limitations.

June 5

Tom failed two subjects. Away went the car again and away went Tom—this time to Northern Michigan.

Tired of travelling the same dusty road again, I pointed out to Mr. King that eventually, whether Tom passed or failed nineteen subjects he would be able to drive a car, even buy one for himself. Why link marks with driving?

November

Tom works part time in a gas station. Interestingly, he wants to be a mechanic and is passing an automotive course in the twelfth grade. Is this one way to train a man to be a mechanic?

"One's position in a group" is called "status," and status is important to all of us—you, me, and most particularly to your adolescent son. A particular ring I wear occasionally makes me feel well dressed; I only wear it when I want to impress someone. Your home, the car you drive, your good necktie, your garden, all contribute to making you feel important to yourself. But you and I know we have fairly important positions as husbands, businessmen, church leaders . . . we have status.

Look at your son's frantic and sometimes agonizing attempts to join groups. He can't make the swimming team because he swims like a rock; he can't date the pretty girl because she won't look at an unpopular non-hero; he has no trouble joining grroups that are weird in behavior but he doesn't want to be weird in behavior; school marks are a constant battle. In his own mind your boy is in a dice game with strangers . . . he has no status.

I see driving as a means for you to accept your boy as an adult and to help him maintain his position in his age group. If your state laws say "sixteen" and you say "Not yet," your son has been put down by you and will be put down by his friends.

Before my sixteen-year-old received his license, we had a little talk, the kind I refer to as a "father-son" talk but the kind he calls a "father-father" talk. Our subject was mainly "Traffic Tickets." (I was at a distinct disadvantage because he had been with me several months before when I had been nailed for failing to come to a complete stop.) I told him to expect an occasional ticket, almost all motorists get them, and when he gets one he is to tell me about it. He is to pay for his own tickets and in the event he gets a serious one, say for reckless driving, he can't drive our car until I say he can.

If he is delayed more than a half hour in arriving home, he is to call. If he has an accident which is his fault, he is to pay the deductible costs. When we finished our one-way discussion, he said, "OK."

So far, so good.

15. CAR THEFT

Few thoughts frighten me more than that of a goofy driver, drunk or sober, totally disabling me or killing me while I'm innocently obeying traffic laws. I see many car thieves in my work and am struck by the lack of remorse of some. To them, it's like the disconnecting of trolley wires we used to do—we kids all knew it was wrong but everybody did it at Halloween.

August 7   "How was it you were riding in that stolen car, Mike?"

"We didn't have anything else to do, Mr. George."

Youngsters with this beginning frame of mind have not proven difficult for us to counsel. They generally have been pretty well racked by parents and police and now have a more adult concept of the potential damage which can be done to other persons' lives with an automobile.

Other youngsters send out smoke signals by stealing cars.

June 5	Terry McHugh, 13, was referred by the court for stealing a car. Throughout our first interview he stared sullenly back at me.
	Widowed Mrs. McHugh gave the impression of complete devotion to her only son. She was always there, like a telephone.
June 15	Terry acted like a stranger who should not have been here at all.
June 24	Ditto.
July 2	Something was stirring in Terry's mind. As if asking for a miracle, he questioned me, "Can you do anything about my mom's drinking, Mr. George?"
	Not too composedly I asked him what he meant.
	"She drinks vodka and hides the bottle under the mattress of her bed. Sometimes she gets actually glassy-eyed when she drinks."
	I then saw Mrs. McHugh alone to ask her about her drinking. She first denied any drinking, but I pointed out that I was not interested in the quantity of liquor she

was drinking but rather in alcohol's effect on her relationships with Terry.

Out came scuttling small, absurd contradictions. She decided to keep the vodka bottle in plain view on the kitchen shelf.

July 15
The McHughs arrived, no longer at odds. Mrs. McHugh was drinking in public, but not too much, and Terry was delighted, like a small child dropping coins in a church collection basket.

Stealing cars may be an indication of deep family financial problems, and the child in his own way may be trying to help his family solve such problems.

May 4
Eddie Leger, 15, thought coming to see me was better than going to jail. He blinked constantly, loved his beer and wine, and was two years behind in school. He yawned his disapproval of me.

The experiences of a lifetime had bleared Mr. Leger's eyes. He had watched with uneasiness for five years while his son stole cars. Mr. Leger was not going to be drawn in.

May 15
Eddie bragged about his gang's organization. They even pre-estab-

lished locations where they could regroup if police stopped them in a stolen car.

I wished I had seen Eddie five years earlier.

May 29

Eddie stated he stole cars to get money—he knew his market for hot carburetors and bucket seats.

Eddie, and then later his mother, told about Mr. Leger's odd concepts about money. He kept a separate bank account, paid no income tax, made his children beg for promised allowance money, shut his wife off from household food money.

Finally Mrs. Leger gave up and went to work as a waitress; at least she would know how much money she could spend for groceries.

There was not much doubt in my mind that Eddie's escort to stealing was his father.

Car stealing may be the simple act of a child who does not understand the damage he can do or it can be an indication of deeper trouble in his relationships with others.

16. SMOKING

The school counselor poured cream into his second cup of coffee. We both were enjoying an insider's conversation about parents and their adolescent children.

"How do you handle the smoking problem?" I asked.

"Did I get blasted the other day," he replied. "I had seen this boy, a junior in our high school, for a routine counseling session, and the day afterwards his mother called me. Her first shot was, 'How dare you offer my boy a cigarette?' I did nothing but listen for several minutes, and then I finally had the chance to say, 'I offer practically everyone a cigarette. Did Larry accept the cigarette and smoke it?' She said, 'No, but you might have been the one to start him smoking,' and wham went the telephone."

"Say, he continued, "can I bum a cigarette from you? I'm out."

"You're cutting into my daily quota," I answered as I handed him one.

There is not much doubt about it ... smoking is damaging to health. On those rare occasions during the past twenty-five years when I've stopped, I've felt better physically but I get irritable, so irritable that my family and friends beg me to begin again. Realize, then, that any thoughts I express about the adolescent smoking problem will be filtered through my own need for smoking.

October 11   Dave Hanson, 15, spoke mostly in silences during our first interview. Along with his important problem of getting tossed out of school for

misbehavior, he and his father had
had a series of angry collisions
about Dave's smoking.

Late in the interview I lit a cigarette and as an afterthought offered
one to Dave. His eyes lit up with
sudden interest—he was being accepted as an adult.

Mr. Hanson was sure that only
gamblers and kept women smoked.
"Dave deliberately disobeys me,"
he snapped.

Some parents think that a child's smoking is a direct
act of rebellion against their authority, but I prefer to
draw the battle lines on a different basis. Children
don't smoke. Many adults, the foolish ones like me,
do. So, it is quite possible that if your son smokes it is
because he wants to think of himself and to have others
think of him as an adult, not a child.

If your son already has the smoking habit you
might as well quit fighting about it because, like driving a car, he will age past your control.

There is another and more interesting side to the
cigarette package: how to prevent a youngster from
starting the habit. Admittedly a father like myself has
a problem when he cautions his son not to smoke while
he lights his own cigarettes end to end, but the situation
is not insurmountable. In my own family I started
talking about the evils of smoking when my older
children were ten, eleven, twelve years old. The expected answer came back, "How come you're talking
this way, Dad? You certainly smoke your share."

My pat answer was, "Remember how difficult it was for you to quit biting your nails and sucking your thumb? Those were habits, too, but you formed them at an age when you were too young to realize what you were doing. Smoking is a habit you deliberately decide to form, and with the weight of medical information telling you it's dangerous, you have more reasons not to smoke than I did twenty-five years ago. I'd like to kick the habit but I'm hooked."

My personal score? An eighteen-year-old daughter, a sixteen-year-old son, and a fourteen-year-old son who have decided not to smoke, but still know that if they were to walk in the house smoking I wouldn't bat an eye. I don't know about that eight-year-old boy of mine: he has a sneaky look sometimes.

17. SEX

Some fifteen years ago, when "Plymouth" meant "a fine car" to prospects, Chrysler Corporation employed a sales manager to tour the country stimulating salesmen to sell more Plymouth cars. A great platform speaker with a fresh carnation always in his lapel, Harry Moock could steam up his audiences to the boiling point. If he were active today he could manage a profitable dealership selling Edsels in Appalachia.

Harry's speeches always came back to the same two points:

1. "Know your product—know more about the Plymouth than any prospect walking into the showroom," and

2. "Believe that you've got the best product on the market today. If you're not convinced that Plymouth builds the best car for the money, go sell something else."

I may seem a long way from sex, a delicate subject, but the same principles prevail when you approach talking sex with your son. How much do you know about sex? Are you convinced that sex is "the best product on the market today?"

Our generation had a curtain around sex: it's a rare adult client I see who knows this product. Here are some written comment from men and women our age:

"Sex—when the opportunity presents itself."

"Sex—I'm not interested right now."

"Sex—I don't know. My wife says I never have enough; I agree with her."

"Sex is something that goes with marriage."

"Sex—nothing, I guess."

"Sex—so-so."

"Sex—yes."

"Sex—I'm not a good bed partner."

"Sex—poor, I guess."

"Sex—should be quite sacred."

Most people our age learned what little they know about sex from sources which usually didn't know what they were talking about. Let's help our children know more about sex and place sex in its proper context within marriage, not as a selfish physical experience pictured in pornographic magazines but more importantly as an emotional experience—the giving of a gift to a loved life partner.

April 23 Mrs. Jones called in tears. The next time I saw Chuck, would I have him explain why he had the dirty magazines under his pillow? I asked her to have Chuck bring in the magazines.

May 1 Chuck dumped the contents of the brown paper sack on my desk—the type of trash displayed on stands of the drug store you don't patronize.

"With your father dead, you've never had a talk about sex, have you, Chuck?"

"I know a little about it, Mr. George."

"Let me give you my slant on sex, then, Chuck. Sex is great . . . for a married couple. Man and woman both play a part in bringing a child into the world, and the act itself is pleasant for the married couple.

"When God made you and me as men, he gave each of us a factory which starts production when you are about 12 to 14; this produces the man's half of the egg necessary to produce a baby. This man's half-an-egg is called a 'sperm.'

"When your factory produces too many sperms, wet dreams result, and a wet dream means that while you're sleeping your penis shoots off the excess production of sperms. Wet dreams are perfectly natural to have and shouldn't bother your conscience because they occur while you're sleeping.

"Let's take a look at a woman's body. Every woman has a factory, too, in which she manufactures her half-an-egg, called an 'ovum.' Combined with your half, her half can create a baby.

"Because a woman carries a baby inside her for about nine months before it is born, her factory is more elaborate. Instead of wet dreams like you have, she gets rid of all her month's production about every thirty days, and then starts getting ready again to have a child.

"You see, Chuck, even today you and the girl you will some day marry are preparing for marriage and the enjoyment of sex.

"You can have intercourse with a woman now, before you marry. Why shouldn't you?

"Within five miles of your home there is probably a prostitute, a woman who sells her body to any man who will pay her to have intercourse with him. If you want to, you can find out her name, see her, and have intercourse with her.

"But notice what is happening if you have intercourse with someone who is not your wife. You are only thinking of intercourse as an action which will satisfy you. Not the woman, just YOU.

"All the emphasis in those magazines is about how great sex is for YOU. They miss the boat completely, because intercourse is mainly an emotional experience and not a physical one. You'd be delighted tonight if your mother were to give you the keys to a new car because she would demonstrate her love for you by giving you a gift. In intercourse, you give yourself to your wife and she gives herself to you. If you think of sex like these magazines do, of only receiving pleasure for yourself, you are not going to enjoy it as much.

"Did I make myself clear, Chuck?"

"Yes, Mr. George," (an answer I anticipated because he was naturally anxious to change the subject).

"Good. Let me repeat what I just told you" . . . and I did.

Chuck waited until I finished, and then asked, "Why shouldn't I read those magazines?"

"Your chances of ending up in bed before you get married increase, Chuck, because such trash is designed to excite you sexually."

The interview was over: he stood up. I said, "Here, Chuck, take these books along with you. I don't want them."

May 16

Near the end of our discussion, I asked, "Chuck, what about the dirty magazines?"

He scratched his head. "I think they're still on the floor of my closet."

Married sex is natural (bees do it) and should not be considered as either the purpose of marriage or the necessary evil of marriage. If you yourself are not enjoying sex I'd suggest a talk with your family physician: he'll cooperate because he sees many sexually frustrated men and women. He'll give you a brief talk like Harry Moock gave the Plymouth salesmen, a talk designed to help you know the product and be convinced that sex IS the best product on the market today.

18. DRINKING

My experience with the teen-aged drunk is limited; most of the young men I've counseled have been of the one shot variety.

What causes a fifteen-year-old boy from a fine home to get smashed suddenly? Perhaps he is simply imitating what his father did.

October 12	Jeff Pappenheim told the story straightforwardly. He had been innocently going to school when a classmate offered him a glass of wine. By 10 a.m. the two were giggling in class.
	When Jeff's parents heard the news, the roof fell in. He was grounded indefinitely.
November 15	Jeff promised to stay out of trouble if only his parents would relent. No go.
December 2	Jeff said he couldn't understand why his parents were being so diffi-

cult. He related one of his family's standing jokes, about the time his father and uncle, at about sixteen, had been sent to their basement to tend the fire, had found a fifth of whiskey, and mixed Calverts with their Coke, shovelling. Jeff's father had been beaten, grounded, and hadn't had a drink in twenty-five years.

Of course, your son may go on the rocks because you enjoy a cheerful glass. If he sees you blossom forth after a drink or two, he may simply want to be happy like you. Without prior imbibing, he may drink too much the first time.

Experts on adolescence claim that this period is characterized by a search for new experiences while the adolescent is trying to establish his own personality. Sometimes sheer boredom will lead a youngster to drink.

December 1 Ed Reynolds, 17, had tossed a brick through a window of an exclusive shop in Bloomfield Hills.

Mrs. Reynolds held two jobs; Mr. Reynolds had deserted his wife and children eight years ago.

I asked Ed, "What happened?" "I got fed up with the same old grind and got drunk, Mr. George."

The steady drinker forgets his personal troubles when he talks pro football or tells dirty stories to the bartender.

August 4 Mrs. Atkinson had trouble waking Mike, 14. He had passed out in a public park near the house.

Patrolman Atkinson's psychiatrist had told him not to carry his gun off duty because of his uncontrollable temper. Mr. Atkinson still carried the gun.

When angered, he would chase Mike around their pool table with a cue in his hand.

I'm sorry for the family in which teetotaling parents look upon alcohol as completely bad. Usually the reason for this attitude is a series of experiences years ago which made today's parents so horrified they can see no good in alcohol. Most adults take an occasional drink—children don't.

Nine years ago "I'll never marry a man who drinks," lovely Kay, 17, told me at a party.

Her parents had driven their attitude into her.

Today Kay teaches school, looks for a husband. Her market is limited because the first time a date orders a brew, he is disqualified.

I've seen families badly disorganized because of drinking. Day after day I hear comments like these:

January 4	"My dad gets drunk every pay day."
August 5	"My dad has three or four highballs after dinner and then just goes to bed."
May 7	"I hide in the closet when my dad comes home loaded."
September 2	"He comes home most nights after I go to bed . . . but I hear the fighting."

As a means of helping your son into adulthood, consider offering him his first drink in your own kitchen, even if you abstain yourself.

In this context, teaching the control of alcohol is one of the most important preparation steps confronting you as a father. What to say? (Step over to the corner of your kitchen . . . perhaps he has a drink in his hand.)

> "Son, you might not like the taste of that Cutty Sark and soda you have, but I think you can probably find some liquor you like; liquor has many different flavors.

"You've seen me drink, even brought me a cold beer from the refrigerator—I never have tried to conceal my drinking from you. You may have noticed that I can come home from work discouraged or angry, have a drink or two with Mother, and relax. That's what drinking does for me, and that's why I have an occasional drink.

"One of the biggest problems you've had as a teen-ager is with me, trying to get me to treat you like an adult instead of the kid you were two or three years ago. And yet, children of ANY age drink excessively ... adults don't.

"If you drink too much, you become like a child; I've seen grown men forget where they left their overcoats, act the same way you used to when you'd ask, 'Where are my mittens?' At any age, even at my age, a man can drink enough to revert to being a child, smack up a car, make a pass at someone else's wife, work poorly because he is hung over.

"Some night soon one of your friends is going to offer you a drink. Don't accept, please, but just watch the behavior of those who do drink. They'll get loud, sing, maybe drive too fast, all things that a kid does, but not an adult.

"If you're in a car and the driver drinks, get out and call me, even if it is four o'clock in the morning. I'll come and pick you up and congratulate you when I do.

"You see, whiskey allows a man to escape problems built into his life. I'm not interested in forgetting my problems; I'm interested in fighting them. The man who drinks excessively is just like you were five years ago when I'd bawl you out for something: childlike, you'd run in and turn on the TV to avoid thinking about the problem."

19. DATING

In our society we often push a teen-ager in two directions at the same time. We quietly, sometimes even stridently, stress the fact that he will only be financially successful if he stays in school, and then undercut our position by worrying if he does not date girls.

November 2

"He's sixteen years old and has never had a date, Mr. George."

"What does he do for entertainment?"

"Well, he's on the school debating team, plays touch football, and shoots a pretty fair game of pool."

I was tempted to ask, "Do you want him to change all his activities so he can get married at about eighteen?"

The adolescent spends time away from home looking for friends, friends with interests like his own. He associates mostly with boys at first, and, as he grows older, he will probably and casually mention, "We all went over to Jennie's house last night." Right then is the time for you to start the screening process, the screening which will eventually lead to your son's selection of a good wife.

"Who's Jennie?" you or your wife can ask. (I think you SHOULD ask.) After getting the information you seek, it is perfectly correct for your wife to call Jennie's mother to thank her for letting your son in her home, check on his behavior, and, most importantly, to form an opinion of how good a parent Jennie's mother is.

October 2

"See if you can convince my folks to let me go over to Cunningham's Saturday night, Mr. George. The whole gang's going." Joe, 16, liked girls.

Later, I asked Mrs. Lang, "How about this party Joe wants to go to Saturday night?"

"Not a chance, Mr. George. He went to one of those parties Jane Cunningham puts on, and when he got home, at 2:30 in the morning, I found out Dr. Cunningham had not been down to the recreation room once during the entire evening. Joe's not going back there again!"

When parents tell me, "I don't know who he goes out with," I hide my dismay; you can bet that if your son is not willing to bring his girl friend home, he knows she won't pass your inspection.

As his model for manhood is you, his model for womanhood is his mother. The girl your son liked most at Jennie's may not be much like your wife, but she is a girl. If your son sees a girl several times, a simple statement like, "I want to meet Judy, son; how about bringing her over to listen to records for a while Saturday night?" should help the screening. If he balks, you can push the meeting by saying, "Look, son, I want to meet this gal of yours. I'll probably like her if for no other reason than the fact that you like her."

Your son's girl friend's sweater may be too tight, her skirt too high, she may chew gum, and besides, you want your son to finish college. You can avoid deep-rooted future problems by being kind to the girl—perhaps she is over-trying to impress you. If you later decide you don't appreciate her talents, you can calmly compare her unfavorably to your wife . . . but later.

September 4 Kevin had an odd story to tell. After months of seeing me regularly to help him get away from his mother's domination, a new problem popped up.

"I'll be on the phone talking to one of my girl friends, Mr. George," he said, "and she'll walk by and say 'don't waste your time talking to THAT drip' loud enough so the girl can hear her. And, she doesn't even know the girl."

It was almost as though Kevin's mother were trying to keep her son from being as unhappy in marriage as she was.

If you toss up your hands and say, "No dating for you at this age," or, worse, act like girls are *verboten*, your son is bound to think, "What's wrong with girls, anyway?"

Problems about your son's dates may rest squarely with your own dating situation years ago. If you were unpopular at the drug store, you may overstress your son's popularity at the drive-in; if you were inadequate in dating beautiful popular girls, you may want him to date only the prom queen; if you were unhappy when dating, you may try to fend off all girls from him.

Dating is a compliment to you and your marriage, after all, because your son wants to imitate you.

20. PART TIME JOBS AND SUMMER JOBS

Several years ago *Time* magazine called the 1960's the "Age of Anxiety." In some senses I agree, but there is also justification for my own name for this era—"The Age of Paper Boys," since I have the conviction that there must be more paper boys than there are paper buyers. Perhaps someone will convince me that delivering papers door-to-door is the great cure-all for adolescent problems.

March 4   George Goodwin, 14, was a stocky youngster with a quick smile and a sharp mind. His immediate problem was a D in algebra. Mr. Goodwin was insisting that George improve in algebra and sell his paper route.

I gave the family the name of an algebra tutor in their neighborhood.

April 2   The tutor was helping, but not enough. Mr. Goodwin was insisting that George stop peddling his papers.

April 18   George brought his average up to
                B in algebra and agreed to sell
                his route . . . then Mr. Goodwin
                changed his mind and insisted that
                George keep the route.

I never did know the well-to-do Mr. Goodwin well
enough to ask whether he had sold papers as a youngster, but I'll bet his answer would have been "Yes."

These young men today are almost universally more
under the pressure gun for marks than we were at
their age; we parents look back and see the valuable
lifetime friendships we ourselves formed in high
school. Do we need to pull our sons away from these
two goals, marks, and friends, toward a couple of dollars a week under the title "business experience" or
"meeting the public"? Part time work during the
school year is a slice of time out of your son's day. Does
he have the time to divert from his main chance?

Summer jobs are also slices of time, but can be
money making training programs for the future. If
your son has attended school thirty hours a week during
the school term, he has thirty extra hours weekly on his
hands come summer. And that thirty hours can be used
to help him answer the question you and I all too frequently ask him, "What do you want to do in life,
anyway?"

October 24   Sylvester, 18, was from the hard-
                est hard core section of the city; he
                dropped out of school because he
                couldn't afford the book costs in

the public schools. He needed a job.

We got him a job in an assembly plant at $88.88 net a week.

December 1   Sylvester came back, out of a job. "What happened?" I asked.

"I just couldn't see myself taking that dust plug out of all those rear axles eight hours a day for the rest of my life, Mr. George. But I need money."

"I don't think you failed, Sylvester; you just learned something I hope you never forget. You are too bright to do work which does not require you to think. Let's find you a job that makes you use your brains, eh?"

Sylvester nodded his head.

If your son were to see you at the office as a stranger and ask the usual question, "Sir, do you need any help around here?" your answer would probably be, "Sorry, young man, we're all filled up." Adolescents have no work experience: where to get it? Younger boys can cut grass or caddy, and older boys can work for your friends in business. (Two friends of mine switched employment of their sons last summer.)

Summer   "I'm proud of Johnny," his father beamed at the cocktail party. "He banked $525.00 this summer."

"What's he going to do with the money, Tom?" his friend asked, dryly.

"Use it to buy clothes for high school and college."

"Not a bad idea. But, couldn't he turn out to be the best dressed drop-out in his school?"

I was impressed several years ago when I overheard a conversation between a young college man and his professor; the student thought his teacher's explanation of a theory was unclear. The young man said, "Sir, I worked construction all last summer to help pay my tuition this year, and I want every dime's worth of the $75.00 I invested in this course." The teacher unbristled and gave a more thorough explanation.

The mother of an eighteen-year-old chuckled as she told us this story—her son came home last summer after his first day's work with the announcement, "Well, Mom, now that I'm working, I won't have to do any more of the household chores. The little kids can do all that."

"Fine, Bill, that's ok with me. Now you and I will talk about room and board."

Innocently, Bill asked, "What's 'room and board'?" The trap snapped shut.

21. TV

Any Day

Although today was the first time I had met Keith, 14, I had met him many times before.

His school counselor had called—Keith, physically in class, mentally was nowhere near the classroom. His mother didn't care how he progressed.

Talking to Keith was not a pleasure; long pauses became a part of our conversation. There was a distinct lack of animation about him, like a bus driver routinely making change.

It was as though he hadn't been with other people long enough to carry on a conversation.

I asked him the question to which I knew the answer, "What do you do when you get home from school?"

"Watch TV."

Someone had slipped Keith a 22" pacifier and forgotten to take it away from him.

TV records some memorable events—we'll all remember President Kennedy's assassination. I've seen Mary Martin, Leonard Bernstein, Richard Burton, Bob Newhart. I've watched Sugar Ray Robinson's combinations, Nicklaus' astounding drives and feathery putting touch, Kaline's complete stardom, Unitas' leadership, Bannister's determined clock-watching. But these outstanding moments only occur once in a black-and-white moon. There is so much quantity and so little quality on TV. If a parent isn't careful, he can allow his set to be turned on all afternoon and evening, with the result that the youngster is unable to distinguish a great show from a time-filler.

November 17   I said, "Tell me about your family dinner hour, Kirk."

"I eat in the living room watching TV."

"Anybody with you?"

"Nope."

Your son is growing older. If you don't check the program he watches, why shouldn't he continue to enjoy Popeye when he is fifteen years old?

October 10   Bob, 15, seemed to be in a twilight zone. Routine events—school attendance, making friends, going out to a show—were insurmountable problems.

After discovering he was a TV man, I asked him what programs he watched.

"Cartoons," he said.

"Tell me about the cartoons you saw last night," I requested.

Bob fell silent; he couldn't remember.

I enjoy watching a show with a youngster and then
drawing him out about what he saw. We recently
watched a program (I think it was quite old because
the planes had open cockpits and the hero kept talking
about strafing the Huns), but my purpose was to make
my young man analyze what he was seeing. So instead
of sitting passively, he was comparing the unfolding
story with his own ideas.

September 10   For the first thirteen years of
Tony's life, his father had been an
alcoholic. For the last two years,
Mr. Bonadeo had been a member
of AA.

"What does your Dad do evenings, Tony?" I asked.

"Nothin', just watches TV."

Granted that Mr. Bonadeo is
home more these days. But, an
element of happiness is still miss-
ing.

Key questions to ask about TV seem to be: Does
this program require active participation by my son?
Is he watching TV because he needs a break from his
homework and enjoyment of an escape laugh or two,
or is he simply filling idle hours, shoving his mind
into a waste-land from which it will be picked up un-
changed in several hours?

22. PHILOSOPHY OF LIFE

(In my most Mitty-like dreams I can't see myself sitting down with one of my sons some night to discuss his philosophy of life . . . or mine either, for that matter. Unlike previous chapters in which we have stressed direct communication between you and your son, this chapter and the next deal more indirectly with your son's development. I request that you read these next two chapters at one sitting.)

By "philosophy of life" I mean your son's basic outlook on where he is headed in this life and the next as well as how his day-to-day activities help him achieve his long-range goals.

When you and I awake in the morning, we generally feel one of three ways about the day to come. Either we are enthusiastic about meeting the opportunities and challenges confronting us today, or we are fearful of our tasks and responsibilities, or we are apathetic and bored with a feeling that life has let us down. Outside events, of course, can make the cheerful man fearful if he knows he is going to lose his job today, or make the bored man whistle because he knows he is leaving on vacation this afternoon.

Our sons are not like us in our comparatively stable outlook on life.

Suddenly he understands what "honesty" is, for example. The pleasure-seeking child who sneaked the candy from the kitchen when no one was looking goes to the other extreme. He searches out examples of dishonesty everywhere around him, relishes catching others in "dishonesty." Just the other night I heard the querulous voice of the teen-ager in my house, screeching, "But, MOTHER, you told me you would have my pants ready so I could wear them to the party!"

Your son must live in a world of many dishonest people—the man who has a mistress, the ticket-fixer, the merchant with money stashed away in hidden escrow accounts, the expense account expert. You can help him gain proper standards by being even more scrupulous in your own honesty, because the youngster who is told to say he is eleven years old at the movie box-office window when he is actually twelve (and therefore should pay the adult rate) is seeing his parents committing, in the youngster's mind, a serious crime.

The young have severe standards.

Most of the adolescent's standards in life will come from his evaluation of how *you* stack up against the ideal standards he develops. I use the following example to show how a son imitates his father's goals:

February 26

I had the time to talk as I walked through the airport lobby but Mike didn't. He waved his hello and kept going.

I've known Mike all my life. He had free use of the family speed boat when he was eleven and enough allowance to patronize a nearby slot machine.

In later years his father bragged how he had made his first million before he was thirty, lost it in the Depression, and then more than recouped.

Mike today is a professional and successful gambler; he travels all over the world, wherever the action is. He drops in unexpectedly with costly presents to visit his five children.

I don't know whether Mike will ever accumulate the fortune his father did: Mike was dealt out of his father's estate.

But, Mike keeps trying.

Some parents get themselves so wrapped up in making a dollar or having dinner served on time they forget to have fun out of life. Naturally, their sons will imitate their parents. Other parents seem to have the one goal in life of being happy; the parents will never make the goal, and their children will also be discontented in their search for elusive happiness.

What should be your son's philosophy of life? Isn't it the gaining, through your help, of a knowledge of those values truly important in his life, and at the same time a knowledge that those values are difficult but interesting to attain?

If you and I can observe our son, in later years, come through a crisis with his eye on the main chance, then, and only then, can we settle back and say, "He turned out beautifully."

23. AWAKENING OF FAITH

Herman Gardens in Detroit is a housing project; in side-by-side apartments live families on welfare, disrupted families, disorganized families. In the project, too, live crime and immorality. About six years ago a man organized a club for about twenty-five fatherless boys there, and the proof that he is the father they need is in the absence of delinquency of the boys and their attendance at weekly meetings. One night recently one of the older boys, now about eighteen, asked the man very seriously, "Ken, tell me. Why should I be good? Almost all the guys around the Gardens are in trouble with the law or chase women. What chance have I got?"

Perhaps the saint in the man, or perhaps the ex-Marine in him, caused him to jab a finger into the youngster's chest. "Because, you s.o.b., this is where God wants you to live to save your soul. You could be living in Bloomfield Hills or Rosedale Park where the living is easy, but those people have their problems, too. This hell-hole," and then he repeated himself, "is where God wants you to live to save your soul."

When you were eight, you had a concrete image in your mind about God. He probably seemed to you to be a bearded, dignified old man who wasn't around very often but who could arrive to solve difficult problems. This concept of God was handed to you by someone else. Now your concept of God, I presume, is that He is not concrete, but abstract. There is a greater distance between you and Him than there was years ago. You arrived at your present concept of God through your own independent research.

How can you best help your own son in the necessary changing of his childhood ideas of God to an adult way of living on this earth with God? Let's talk about us parents, first.

I agree with the priest who wrote, "As I ascend the altar to say Mass each morning, the daily battle between distraction and devotion begins."

You and I can become so embroiled with the problems of life, because life is so daily, that we don't often think of God. Our impressionable sons then can assume that God is not important for them, either. If you wish, you may follow what one of my clients did—he pasted a two minute prayer on the mirror of the only bathroom of his house. When he shaves, he tries to remember to say the prayer, and when he forgets, he remarks to his family that he has forgotten to say it. The prayer points out his relationship to God: ". . . I offer You my prayers, works, joys and sufferings of this day." The father benefits because everything he does that day is for God, and the family sees that Dad doesn't really run the family, God does.

Another father blesses his children at night-time and sometimes they get to bed before he touches them on their foreheads. His fourteen-year-old son asked him one night recently, "What are you saying, Dad, when you bless me as I'm falling asleep?"

His father replied, "I say 'May the Lord bless you and keep you from all evil. Amen.' "

The adolescent grunted and rolled over in his bed.

If you believe as I believe, that faith is a growing toward God on a day-to-day basis, that your own faith is sporadically but generally becoming stronger, and that as you grow older you are more able to forgive those who trespass against you, your own love of God will positively influence the religious awakening of that beguiling son of yours. For, as a theologian once said, "A child will not love God unless he loves the person who teaches him that love."

24. RELIGIOUS DOUBTS

Flatly the professor said, "All adolescents encounter religious doubts."

I thought back to my own adolescence years ago and made the mental reservation, "He's generalizing again; I never had any religious doubts when I was a teen-ager."

Then the teacher backed off. "The brighter the adolescent, the more chance he will have to encounter these religious doubts."

I had been put in my proper intellectual place.

Through your son's earlier years, you were like God to him: when you spoke it was Gospel and when you showed him you liked him it was like Christ saying, " . . . and the greatest of these is charity." Lately, he may be becoming more sensitive to the intangible goals you value highly. He may find a few chinks in your armor where they don't exist; his greater sensitivity to the problems of the world can supply the first reasons why a young man develops religious problems.

June 17   "Why is there so much suffering in the world if God loves us?" the serious young man asked me.

In the preceding chapter we talked about the way an adolescent's method of thinking changes. Sometimes as he steps from one sidewalk square to the next, he stubs his toe.

November 10   John, 16, was tossed out of a parochial high school for truancy.

A silent enigma, he would only answer direct questions and could state no reason why he skipped.

Whenever I asked John a question, his father, self-assured and self-confident, leaped in with the answer.

December-   John settled down to attend school.
February   We were ready to stop seeing each other when he mentioned, with a devout wish to cooperate, that he did not believe in the existence of God.

Religious doubts may occur when the teen-ager's parents tell him one path to take and then take another path themselves.

October 9   Dave Godderis, 15, resented coming to see me. Among his exploits was the time he was caught displaying a switchblade in the school rest room. He wouldn't attend Mass on Sunday.

Authority to Dave was something to be automatically reacted against.

I asked Mrs. Godderis how often she attended church herself.

"Oh," she said, seemingly startled by my question, "I was married before to another man, so I don't go to church."

Perhaps Mrs. Godderis, in not complying with her own chosen authority, was demonstrating the point to Dave.

March 16

Roger, 12, was a freckle-faced little leprechaun who calmly stated he couldn't care less about school. He was capable of B work but was getting D's.

Another parochial school student, he didn't like any part of the school discipline imposed on him.

"How often do you get to Mass?" I asked him.

"Our school goes every day, Mr. George, and so do I."

"How often do your parents go?"

Judging from his answer, his
parents' religious beliefs were outside his ken. "Oh, they go every
Sunday, but they never receive
Communion. And, they won't tell
me why."

As your son trots through the living room with a
Coke in his hand, it would be extremely unlikely that
he would say over his shoulder to you, "Guess what,
Dad, I don't believe there IS a God." More than likely
he will keep any confusing religious doubts, if they
arise, to himself. So, there is nothing untoward in your
comment to him, "It's not too rare, I understand, son,
for young men your age to have religious doubts. If
you get them, mention them to me, will you?" If
you set up hurdles for your son in his search for God,
he may trip.

October 9   Mr. Schroeder's religious beliefs
were an iron-bound scripture from
which any deviation was sinful.
Richard, 17, was not sure God
existed.
"I told him, Mr. George, I told
him. I said, 'Richard, you are going right straight to hell unless you
start believing in God.'"

If you are firm in your religious beliefs, it might be
well not to get involved in an eyeball to eyeball con-
frontation with your son, should he develop doubts.
It would be better to take him for a walk some starry

evening and point out to him how some of the constellations, for example the Hunter, the Twins, the Dragon, had their names bestowed on them so long ago that their namers are unknown, and yet every year on this particular night the constellations are in exactly their same places above us. Someone smarter than man, more powerful than man, put those stars there.

Like deliberately leading a duck in flight with a shotgun blast, knowing that the duck and the pellets will meet, we shoot satellites far off the track to the moon, knowing that satellite and moon will converge months from now. Man doesn't make the moon move over, naturally, but he has recently become intelligent enough to compute a faint trace of God's intelligence.

Religious doubts are usually positive developments; they are another expression of your son's striving to be independent. Like the verbal hostility we discussed in another chapter, the more independent (and intelligent, I guess, from what the professor said) your son is, the more prone he will be to wonder about the existence of God.

3
School Situations

25. IQ

My oldest son loped into the kitchen one evening last summer. "Guess who I caddied for today, Dad—Bruce Maher!" (Maher is a defensive safety man for the Detroit Lions pro football team. He is a sure tackler and an excellent pass defender.)

"How did he play?" I asked.

"Tremendously long off the tee, Dad, and his irons are good, too. Funny thing, though. He can't putt. He three-putted about six greens and even four-putted number twelve." My son talked as though he and the football player shared a private joke between them.

As Maher has fairly obvious strengths and weaknesses in golf, so probably does your son in his intelligence, his IQ.

Will you dig out your boy's last report card?

His report card is a record of your son's ACHIEVEMENT, what he has already done in competition with his classmates. Marks on the report card are a matter of record like election results—nothing can be done to alter either.

Some teen-agers work at top capacity but most don't. If you are content with your son's marks, you can skip reading the rest of this section. If, however, you believe your son can do better in school marks than he is now doing, please continue reading because I believe you, your son, and I can improve his marks.

Please remember, though, that if he has a C IQ and you demand A's, misbehavior and underachievement may result from the pressure YOU apply.

April 28	Mrs. Bryan called to ask us to see her son, George. George had the highest IQ in his class at a private high school but was failing. He had stolen small sums of money from his mother.
	George's school advisor informed me that George had four F's and a D on his last report card. Group counseling sessions (four or five boys with problems similar to those of George airing their mutual problems with an advisor) had not been effective. George would agree with the group aims and then do what he wanted to do—fail.
May 5	George came in like a stranger who should not be seeing me at all. He was completely uncommunicative except to answer direct questions.
	Mrs. Bryan could not understand why George, the brightest boy in the class, was failing.
May 15	George lay practically on his spine throughout his interview.

He thought coming to see me was a waste of time like the group counseling sessions at school.

June 2

I started off our session today with the statement, "I really don't think you're the genius your mother tells me you are." George straightened in his chair and shot back, "You know, I don't think I'm particularly brilliant either."

We discussed a recent group IQ test he had taken in which he had ranked at the eighty-eighth percentile. In other words, he was better than 88% of the students who had taken the same test. We agreed that 88% should result in B and C marks.

I then showed his mother, in the small print of the same test, how George was bright but not brilliant.

It's now fall, and I've only seen George twice since June, but he called the other day to tell me his marks: 2 B's, 2 C's, and a D in auditorium. I asked him how anyone could get a D in auditorium ... he laughed as though he had been caught crashing the gate at a school dance.

His mother is content with his

B's and C's; he has not stolen anything lately.

I may have created the impression that once an IQ score is attained, your son has been pigeon-holed. Not so. Any IQ test searches for knowledge acquired by the testee.

April 20

Pat McLeod, 13, came to see me because he had skipped 26 days of school this semester.

His mother had recently had a baby which was put out for adoption immediately. She had been separated from her husband for years.

Pat earned his living shining shoes for business men in his neighborhood.

I had the impression he was a shrewd business man himself, and so administered a standard intelligence test to Pat.

If Pat had scored a 100 on this test, he would have indicated that his intelligence was average.

He shot 112.

But later, while discussing his examination with him, I mentioned the word "carpenter." He interrupted me to ask, "What's a carpenter?"

It should not be surprising to hear about another boy who spent the first twelve years of his life in a modern inner-city ghetto; his IQ was so low he was sent to a training school to equip him for some simple career, like sweeping the streets. Four years later his IQ was tested again and his measure of intelligence had jumped all the way up to average.

One point seems important—your son's IQ, admittedly a nebulous figure, probably will not decrease unless he has a brain damaging accident or runs into emotional problems which prevent him from concentrating.

As he acquires the right type of knowledge, your son's IQ can increase.

26. IQ AND TEACHERS

In our continuing search for your son's IQ, we are now looking for a specific person—the man or woman at your son's school who knows most about him and his educational abilities. Our wanted man may be a home room teacher, a counselor, or a principal. Whatever his title, he has some facts and opinions you can use profitably.

Your son can give you the name of the teacher who knows him and his work best. I suggest that you call the teacher and make an appointment to see him privately. Ask him to have your son's school records available when you see him.

These records can be helpful to you because schools nowadays are "test-happy." Flourishing companies write all sorts of tests; they then sell the tests to schools around the country, administer the tests and compare individual scores. If your teacher tells you your son "scored at the seventy-fifth percentile" in a particular test, the information is probably valid because this same test has been administered to thousands of youngsters of the same age and school grade throughout the nation.

A word of caution. Many of these tests are written by research educators for their own experimentation— you and I as parents are not considered. Instead of giving results is language we understand, educators obtain results in language they understand. If your son were to score a 98 on a Stanford-Binet test, you might feel like bragging a little, but you'd be wrong. On this test a 98 would indicate your son's intelligence is just about average.

So, your first question after the teacher tells you your son's test scores might be, "How does he rank with all the others who took the same test?"

A follow-up question might well come to your mind when you consult the teacher—"How valid is this man's opinion of my son?"

I believe the teaching profession has many more good apples and many more bad apples than most professions. An automobile mechanic is usually either extremely capable or average; the poor mechanic cannot make a living. Not so in the teaching profession because the poor teacher is seldom replaced.

Here is an example of a teacher whom I think should either be replaced or sent back to school for further training:

May 6   Mr. Galvin called to ask for an appointment for his son, Jim, 11. Jim was misbehaving in school. Mr. Galvin broke down in tears when telling me a teacher had described Jim as "slightly spastic."

May 18   Jim walked in as though he had been here before. There was no sign of the uncontrollable gestures of a spastic. He played ball on his class team this spring.

     Mr. and Mrs. Galvin, worrying without a cause, were relieved when I stated I thought there was nothing physically wrong with Jim. Who wouldn't be?

     I asked them about Jim's teacher—she was brand new in the profession.

Please don't misunderstand what I'm saying. I believe one of my own children won a partial high school scholarship because his seventh grade teacher was so helpful to him.

April and May   I spent many hours with Doug, 14, and his parents. I heard a woeful recitation about six adults—his parents, grandparents and two un-married uncles—all living in the same house and all telling him what to do and what not to do. Doug became confused. Once his mother found him with a dog chain around his neck, ready to commit suicide.

Doug's situation finally im-proved, thank heaven, but while I was working with him, his teacher, Mrs. Williams, called me fre-quently.

Sentiments of hers like, "the poor dear," "or I spent an hour and a half after school last night with Doug, going over his his-tory," and "the saddest youngster I've seen in thirty years of teach-ing," indicated to me that Mrs. Williams was a gem of a teacher.

Your evaluation of the teacher may be summed up by asking yourself, "Does this man like his work?" If he demonstrates to you that he likes your son and his own profession, you can value his opinions. If not, you must look further for some qualified person to help you find your son's intellectual strengths and weaknesses.

27. FINDING SIMPLE ANSWERS FIRST

The little boy's mother had read enough about psychiatric theories to know Sigmund Freud's emphasis on dreams. She asked me to investigate why her son was having so many nightmares. I conducted the boy's interview, waiting very cleverly until just before he left to ask him, "Had any scary dreams lately?"

"Only when I see those horror movies on TV," he replied.

I keep reminding myself of the nightmare story. Often the cause of misbehavior or underachievement may be a quite simple one.

September 8   I saw Chuck Giradello, a fifteen-year-old car thief, who told me firmly and precisely that he intended to quit school as soon as he was sixteen, work a year laying sod, and then join the Marines.

Struck with his maturity, we gave him an IQ test. The ninth grader had third grade reading ability. His classmates called him "Stupid."

After four months with a reading clinic, his reading skill was up to the ninth grade. He was planning to finish high school.

Call your own son into the room, if you will. Hand him the sports page of the daily newspaper and ask him to read a paragraph ALOUD. Judge whether he reads satisfactorily. Does he hold the newspaper at normal distance from his eyes?

Often a specific subject will give a youngster trouble, dragging down all of his marks while he struggles with the one difficult course.

October 12	Tim McCarthy, 14, a bright little sparkler, was failing algebra in the ninth grade. He was spending so much time on his math that his other subjects were suffering.
	Tim's father's directions were simple but improper: "Study harder."
	I suggested to Mrs. McCarthy that they obtain a tutor for Tim. She found a graduate student in a neighboring college who was majoring in mathematics.
	In four sessions, Tim liked modern math; he had a C average.

You might also profit from this example:

September 23	John Polito, 16, refused to go to school because the youngsters called him a "queer."
September 26	John was a dark-skinned swarthy young man of Italian extraction. I could detect no signs of effeminacy. He talked freely, frankly

about his situation. Comments about his masculinity had gotten to him so much he was on tranquilizers and sleeping very little.

John had a habit I had never observed before of suddenly losing eye contact and dilating his eyes above my head.

We spent some time together in front of the mirror in the men's room—perhaps this simple affectation was causing the comments from his peers.

October 10

A completely relaxed youngster walked in.

John's eyes did not lose contact once during the interview.

He has been sleeping nine hours a night without tranquilizers.

28. SCHOOL DISCIPLINE

The school principal, picking his words with precision, reduced the problem of school discipline to a workable framework, at least in my mind, with these words:

I am going to talk to you parents tonight about discipline and I know you will be pleased to hear that my speech will be brief.

I believe that disciplining your child is your responsibility and that when you send your child to this school, you ask us to discipline your child.

I use discipline in this way—I expect a child to obey me when I tell him to do something or punish him for misbehaving. I expect him to obey me whether he believes the punishment is just or unjust. I will discuss the justice of his punishment with him (or you parents if you wish to call me) only AFTER the child has obeyed me.

After deliberately, inflexibly stating his position, the principal sat down. He seemed startled by the ringing applause received.

Discipline is "training that strengthens." A friend recently told me about a Marine sergeant who took gloomy satisfaction in punishing enlisted men under his command. When his platoon was trapped at the Changhin Reservoir in Korea, the Marines knew they had to feel their way to safety. The sergeant ordered his men to stay with him, not to search for individual escape routes. The platoon stayed together . . . reached safety. One of the men injured was the sergeant. His men dragged him to safety. The platoon had had that "training that strengthens."

Lest I be accused of suggesting that you send your son to a reform school tomorrow morning, let me elaborate. I've seen too many adolescent boys unnecessarily in rebellion against school discipline. Parents sometimes dump a boy on the doorstep of the school and leave him to find out what the school rules are after he gets in trouble.

June 8   I saw Tom Applegate and then later his mother. Tom was a "grease," complete with long hair, pointed suede shoes, and tight-fitting black pants. Tom's friends, outside of school hours, were also "greases."

The high school Tom attends will not allow a boy to be a "grease." School authorities insist on "frat" attire, brush haircuts, light-colored trousers.

Tom was failing school.

I'd like to discuss a term here which we have used frequently throughout this book. The term is "preparation" which means "to make mentally ready." How much simpler Tom's life would have been for him if his parents had prepared him, made him mentally ready, to accept the school discipline before he ever attended high school. His father could have made simple comments like, "Tom, notice how sharp Jack looks with that short haircut they wear nowadays—he certainly looks like a man and not like a girl"; or, "Tom, it seems to me those pointed shoes would be O.K. when you're horseback riding but not in a high school class room." These comments would have been effective IF they were made when Tom was a sixth or seventh grader—before he had friends of his own who wore "grease" clothing.

By the time Tom came home from high school with pointed shoes and uncut hair, he had made up his own mind that "points" and long hair gave him status with friends he wanted to impress. His parents had been caught unprepared.

I suggest that you find for yourself the disciplinary rules in your son's school and, by all means, back up the school rules.

May 29	Mrs. Jackson called. Eddie, 11, was failing the sixth grade. Eddie's nun told Mrs. Jackson she was spoiling her son. Mrs. Jackson had the edges of impatience in her voice when relaying the teacher's advice.
June 24	Mr. and Mrs. Jackson came in to explode their many bombs about the horrible nuns at St. Anne's School. They had an argument between themselves about which one hated the nuns more. Mr. Jackson remembered that when he was a child his nun would not let him leave class to go to the bathroom.
July and August	I saw this family several times and suggested that the child should be enrolled in a public school.
Fall	Mr. Jackson called the other day to brag about Eddie's five B's and an

A on his report card at a public school.

Sometimes I ask parents to write their own opinions about different topics. Here is a sampling of some of the opinions about the disciplining of children:

"It's very good until adolescence."

"I try to, but sometimes can't."

"I am tough."

"We take away privileges."

"I am confused."

"I do not discipline them enough. I let them get away with a lot because I am not with them."

"We try to talk to them first."

"It's easy to do but I'm getting laxer at it."

"It's very hard."

"I never know whether I'm doing the right thing."

"Sometimes I may be too strict on my son. My wife thinks I am."

"We (my wife and I) do not agree."

"Ugh! I open my mouth too much and my husband judges them as a group."

In the minds of these parents, "discipline" has become "punishment." If you think that discipline is the same as punishment, you will resent the school rules. If you think of discipline as "training that strengthens," discipline becomes a positive thing. Your son will reflect your attitude.

29. HOMEWORK

You, Dad, can help your son improve his homework. I promised in the introduction of this book not to use technical language, so I'll express my thoughts about learning this way. Your son's marks will improve if you follow, in sequence, these five steps:

1. Expect his homework to be done regularly.
2. Check his homework with him when completed.
3. Immediately praise him for his efforts.
4. Let ten minutes of time pass by.
5. Then, calmly show him his mistakes.

Praise and the time element are vital to improvement. My eight-year-old son showed me a composition the other night; the first thing I noticed at the top of the page was his name—he had transposed two letters. Instead of "Joseph George" he had written "Joseph Goerge." If I had crammed this thoughtless error down his throat immediately, undoubtedly he would have balked on doing other needed corrections on the paper. It took me about thirty seconds to find something to praise him for. (I complimented him for the imagination he had used in his writing.) He went away to take a break. After ten minutes, I picked up his composition again and asked, with a smile on my face, "Joey, how do you spell 'George'?"

He looked at the papers as if for the first time and whistled, "Gee, Dad, I'm glad you caught that mistake. Mrs. Jackson would have blown her stack." He was well prepared to accept my corrections for other mistakes he had made.

Let's apply this psychological principle to you. You finish a project at work and you know it's good. Your supervisor comes along and says, "That's excellent. That's as good a piece of work as we've turned out in months."

Recall how his full and immediate praise affects you. If he praises you the next day, you don't feel as elated as you would have been the day you finished the work. If your supervisor accepts your best efforts with no comment or immediately criticizes them, you lose your desire to perform well.

Let's get back to the five specific steps. Step 1 was "Expect his homework to be done regularly."

Nothing turns a boy against homework so absolutely as parental nagging. Your boy should not have to think of your home as just another classroom.

July 24

I saw Jerry Broehm, a bright undersized youngster of 15. In an oddly neutral and reflective way, he told me about his school. He does well except for Algebra and French. These subjects he was taking for the third time in summer school.

His father maintained what Jerry called the "C Level." If Jerry averaged C's, no trouble. If not, he was grounded until the next report card.

Mr. Broehm was a fireman. After many years away, he decided last February to re-enter college.

Mr. Broehm had 2 D's on his first report card. (I held back my question about whether Mr. Broehm had grounded himself after his first report card.)

August-October I saw the family several times but was unable to prevent Mr. Broehm from forcing Jerry to study. He even stopped Jerry from obtaining a driver's license because of bad marks.

Jerry took an IQ test which indicated he was easily capable of A and B work.

November Jerry was waiting for me when I arrived at work; he looked uncertain and sad.

He had run away from home, spent the night on the back seat of a wrecked automobile to stay out of the snow. He flatly refused to go home.

I parked Jerry in a YMCA near his home for the night, and the next day negotiated a deal with his parents. Part of the package was that Mr. Broehm would not nag his son about homework.

Jerry went home. Whether this
bright boy will complete high
school or not is a question.

"Expecting his homework to be done regularly,"
then, is calmly asking your boy, "How much homework
do you think you should do each night to obtain the
marks you want this school year?"

Let him think over his answer. He may surprise you
and say, "Two hours a night." Then, of course, you
say, "O.K., lets see if you can finish your work satisfactorily in two hours a night. If you can, well and
good."

Get up and walk away. Your boy has made an agreement with a man he dearly wants to please—you. As
long as he puts in that two hours a day between the
time he comes home and the time he goes to bed, you
have no complaints . . . until or if his marks drop. Then
you can say, "Son, do you think two hours of homework a night are enough to do the job?" He will commit himself to the proper time necessary.

If you force your son to do his homework at times
you specify, he'll rebel as surely as you do when, for the
fifth time, your wife asks you to replace the front hall
closet light bulb.

Under steps 2 ("Check his homework with him
when completed.") and 3 ("Immediately praise him
for his efforts."), I suggest you tell your son first that
you want him to show you his homework each night
and that you expect him to show you his good efforts.

April 10   I saw Andrew Galt, 11. He was
                           failing four subjects. He had been
                           tested and had a high IQ.

April and May	I saw Andrew and his mother several times. Mrs. Galt had a dominant hostility toward her boy. My main point was to ask Mrs. Galt to praise her son for his school efforts.
May 25	Andrew walked in like a visiting monsignor. "I only had four words wrong out of fifty on a spelling test, Mr. George," he said.
	I congratulated him. Later I asked his mother what she had said when Andrew brought home his spelling test. She replied, "I told him, 'That's fine, Andrew. Why wasn't it a 100%?' "

The lady had praised her son, then immediately removed all the benefits by not letting ten minutes go by before criticizing him.

May 6	Tom told me he had every answer correct on a geography test.
	"What did your parents say?" I asked.
	"Nothing."
	I felt as though Tom had been cheated.

My last step to better homework is "Calmly show him his mistakes." I should add, ". . . if you are a capable teacher." In math, modern or old-fashioned, my children lose me at about the fifth grade.

In your case, if you know more about the subject than your son does, and can praise him, stay with him. Otherwise, please keep your temper down and get better results by finding a tutor who does know more about the subject than your son!

30. UNDERACHIEVEMENT

Recently we stopped to visit some friends we had not seen for a long time. After drinks, the conversation veered to school marks and to the popular term "underachievement." (In my school days, and probably yours, there was no such thing as underachievement—we simply passed or failed.) In the last thirty years "standardized tests," the same test administered thousands of times to children of the same age, have been sold to school boards around the country. Whoopee! We can now compare our sons with other children as a golfer fights for a par or a bowler tries for a strike in each frame. Are we further ahead or have we fallen into another educator's trap? Are parents unnecessarily driving children to good marks because somebody says he can do better than he is now doing?

Webster says an underachiever is "a student who does not accomplish as much in school as is expected from his measured intelligence." In other words, authors of these standardized tests maintain that they can validly test your son. The tests, however, make no measure of such important test factors as whether your son had been up the night before with a sore throat, whether he had wrenched a knee playing basketball the day before, whether he heard you come home stoned the night before, whether he had just argued with his best girl friend, or whether he just couldn't see the importance of exerting himself the day of the intelligence test.

I deliberately watched my finger clinking the ice cube in the glass and commented to our friends, "You know, I sometimes think there is no such thing as an underachieving child."

"I'll show you Joe's school records," my host shouted.

"I doubt the validity of the records."

"Well, explain what you mean, Bill."

I changed the subject. I did not want to antagonize our friends. I will add that the husband is no amateur with a shot glass.

Children often underachieve because of family situations outside the classroom.

April 3   One would have had to look several times at Mr. Harrison to note that he was expensively dressed. A sensible and serene man, he was concerned about his son's marks.

Mr. Harrison's own background was interesting—at twenty-one he had become vice-president of his family's business which had promptly gone bankrupt in the Depression. Mr. Harrison had refinanced; today he is accumulating his second million dollars.

His seventeen-year-old son, Bill, had the social manners of the very wealthy. He worked just hard enough at high school to get through, then planned to attend an easy college and join the family business.

April 24

I asked Mr. Harrison more about his business. Without throwing his pride around he stated he could retire tomorrow if he wished. I asked him, "How much reading do you do?"

"I read my correspondence and my own financial statements."

"Nothing else?" I asked.

Like a craftsman coolly assessing the field of action at hand he replied, "I don't have to."

I slipped the knife in. "Neither does Bill—he's set for life without cracking a book."

Although Mr. Harrison smiled, it was a reproof: he was not pleased.

I'm convinced that the most important step you as a parent can take to help your son's interest in learning is to be interested in learning yourself. If you tell your son to study and you don't study yourself, he's trapped. Should he follow your words or your actions?

The "Corporation Man," I believe, can trap himself and his son into underachievement simply because the father is so immersed in corporation life that he not only works days but also evenings to advance himself "corporation-wise."

May 2	Sixteen years ago, Mr. Hadly clerked for General Motors. Now he heads an important department. Mr. Hadly, in what might have been the last in a long line of sermons, related how he soon discovered the more time he spent with his superiors the faster were his promotions.
	His friends today are almost entirely GM executives; they build cars and cut production costs over the card table.
	"When was the last time you took a constructive interest in Joe's marks?"
	He squirmed in his chair.
April 11	Mr. Johnson was an electrical contractor who started his own business years ago. He is now successful enough so he can take time to be with his boy, but does not be-

cause he enjoys his own business acumen.

I wondered whether Mr. Johnson had conduits instead of veins and arteries.

Friction at home sometimes causes a son's school underachievement. The boy who hears a shouter going on between parents across the breakfast table is hardly in a frame of mind to conjugate a Latin verb.

May 2 Tony's voice held a curious note of resignation when he stated, "Everybody fights at our house."

July 7 Mrs. Gannon, in embarrassment, explained that her husband wants sexual intercourse much more frequently than she does.

  He was building a trailer in their garage, working late into the night, only coming into the house to browbeat his wife and three sons.

This business of underachievement has many sides. If some of my examples strike close to your home, you have two choices: either correct your own situation as much as you can or accept your son's underachievement. I hope you see why I'm tempted to say (as I wanted to tell our friends), "There's no such thing as an underachieving child ... parents underachieve!"

31. DROP-OUT

The padlock on the front door of my dad's Ford dealership was colder than the zero weather; he was bankrupt. Prolonged delay in producing the 1929 model "A" Fords, refusals by the factory to allow him to cut his overhead expense, a dribble of the hot new cars, had put him close to the financial wall. Then came the Depression and the only employe he had left was his oldest son who stayed because there was no place else to go.

"What do we do now, Dad?"

Without bothering to straighten his shoulders or stick out his chin, my dad replied, "Son, let's go find some automobiles to sell."

As the father of a son who has dropped out of school, you are undoubtedly concerned. Let's constructively help you rebuild your hopes and dreams . . . let's find some automobiles for YOU to sell.

Perhaps after all, God did not give your son the intelligence to pass his school subjects.

April 5   Big Darryl Kohanski smiled because that was what he liked to do. His marks were consistent—all F's.

His mother simply could not understand why Darryl at 16 was not doing better. Yet any minor suggestion of mine led to her automatic question, "Is THAT the problem?"

Mr. Kohanski bowled five nights a week. He went through the eighth grade himself.

June-October   Darryl had many downs, few ups. He wanted to drop out of school but his father threatened to toss him out of the house if he did drop out.

He skipped school, was caught stealing 25 cents from another student's locker, was told to drop out.

We helped Darryl get a job delivering blueprints on foot. He's making $1.30 an hour, happy as a lark.

Another possibility to consider is that your son is bright but unmotivated, a condition which probably has existed for several years. I've already discussed cases of this type in the "Underachievement" chapter, and so I suggest you calmly accept the fact that he is out of school, get him some aptitude tests to find what HE would like to do in life, and do your damnedest to help him get a job in that field. He may find he is too bright for the job he gets and make his own choice to go back to school.

Or, your son may develop a severe and sudden emotional problem.

October 5   When John Tindall, 15, started high school, he began having migraine headaches which kept him out of school more than half the time.

You name the medical examination—he has had it. Physically, he was fine.

October 20 After John missed an appointment I called his house. His mother said he could not get out of bed.

My advice to her was to call her family physician to ask him to refer John to a psychiatrist, fast.

The boy who drops out of school loses an activity which has been a major part of his life for ten to fifteen years. Unable to admit it, he is lost; he has no place to go except home. You don't help his confusion by screaming over spilled credit hours.

November 24 George Holland's high school career ended the day he asked his instructor to help him weld a handle on a long knife he had made. The school principal administered the *coup de grace*—out went George.

George called from a telephone booth downtown, asking, "What do I do now? My mother says I'm finished at home, too."

I asked him to sit tight while I called his mother.

Mrs. Holland calmed down.

I called George back and told the youngster that he could go home.

On his own, George decided to continue at another school. I think the shock of getting tossed out woke him up.

The drop-out has proven to himself and perhaps even to his parents that he does not do well in a formal classroom situation. Please make the best of the situation and help your son search for some work which will help fill the hours that school used to fill. He needs you desperately.

32. VIOLENCE

I can imagine the setting. One of Hitler's lieutenants rushed into Berchtesgaden one day and said: "I think I have figured out a way to get rid of the Jews."

"How?" Hitler asked.

"We make them a group despised by 'good' Germans. In the beginning, we encourage Germans to destroy the Jews' property, and then the Germans will learn to destroy the Jews physically."

"What do we accomplish?" Hitler asked.

"First, the Nazi party makes money because we seize all property confiscated from the Jews. Secondly, the party will save money because civilians will learn to do our police work for us. Thirdly, we train our Aryans to be violent, so that when we are ready to conquer the world, our people will be accustomed to anger in the streets."

"Your first two points are obviously good," Hitler commented, "but you lost me on that point about 'violence.' How can we train a passive group of people like Germans to be violent?"

The aide continued. "We publicly praise acts of violence against the Jews, and the Germans will start trying to out-do each other in acts of violence against them. Everybody is capable of violence, my Fuehrer, because people in authority issue orders to those under them, orders which anger the underlings. We encourage the underlings to take out their anger against the Jews. Look at it this way—an eighteen-year-old Aryan clerk gets angry at his supervisor. As it is now, he can do nothing to dissipate that anger; he can't take a punch at the supervisor. We encourage the clerk to spit in the face of the next Jew he meets. He tranfers his anger from his supervisor down to someone who cannot retaliate against him."

If you remember the post-war trials of the Nazis, you were amazed at the number of seemingly decent Germans who were involved in exterminating six million Jews. Hitler, embarked on his genocidal course, had taught the Germans to transfer their natural feelings of anger into violence against a race which could not fight back.

May 22

Jerry Campbell, 13, had clipped an acquaintance with a clothes pole.

Jerry was almost six feet tall. He lived alone with his divorced mother, a tiny woman needing high heels to reach five feet in height.

I waited about half the interview before asking the key question. "Jerry, who has been hitting you?"

"My mother."

I probably showed my amazement when I asked, "With her hand?"

"No. With a rubber overshoe."

"How often?"

"Four or five times a week."

Mrs. Campbell, a tiny dictator, was training her son well. He could transfer his anger at her to someone below him in the social pecking order.

There is a basic difference between the corrective pat on the fanny given to the four-year-old who has to be taught to stay out of the street and the beating given to the teenager who has come home an hour later than scheduled. Rage is present in the hand of the man who uses weapons like these—electric light cords, rubber hoses, pool cues, razor straps, belts, clothes lines, wooden ladles, and tire chains. Your rage damages your son because it establishes anger at you in your son's mind and yet your son cannot diminish his anger by striking back at you. His anger, planted by you, then may blossom forth in hostility toward someone he can attack with relative impunity.

June 17
The little ten-year-old was another one of those I would have liked to take home with me for keeps.

"Your dad gets drunk and beats you almost every night?" I asked.

"Yep, Mr. George," he declared.

And then he added, as though he were proud of his accomplishment, "But I don't mind too much —I get to beat up my little sister."

Sometimes there is no one for the underling to kick down at. There is no one younger than or smaller than he, or he knows that there would be too much parental retaliation, hell to pay, if he were to show the violence he feels. What does he do? Simple . . . he just waits for his own children to come along and is violent to them.

December 20
"My father," the middle-aged man asserted, "ruled our family with an iron hand. When he told us to do something, man, we moved. Either that or get beaten with a rubber hose."

Deliberately, maliciously, sadistically, this same client beat his little

boy every morning "to get him
out of bed."

How can the chain be broken, how can you prevent
your son, if you have taught him violence, from show-
ing his violence to his younger brothers or sisters or
his school acquaintances?

When grown men brawl on the street, they act like
kids: when you beat your son, you act like a kid.

Your main goal with your son is to help him become
a grown-up man.

4
Family Situations

33. THE LARGE FAMILY

The cold ham and potato salad were just about gone. Our wives and some of the older children were cleaning up the picnic site while the younger children walked a log from one bank to the other. Ed's baby, on a blanket, looked up at the clouds.

"Ed," I began, "your children are about a year or two older than mine, generally, and I've been watching your success raising them. What's your secret?"

"So far, Bill," he said, "they're doing pretty well, I'll admit. Just the other night Ellen and I were agreeing that this particular summer may be the one we look back on in years to come, remembering that at THIS time the children were all doing well."

"How do you maintain the close relationship you have with your children?"

"Sometimes it's not too close. Young Eddie isn't here today. What Ellen and I try to do, though, is to spend individual time with each child."

"Every day?"

"No, it can't be scheduled that exactly."

"For example, what did you do last night with your children individually?"

Ed paused to remember. "Well, I made popcorn and lost a game of 'Old Maid' to Johnny; I lost a table hockey match with Mike, but I did take him to overtime for a change; I listened to three Beatle records with Ann, who was sick in bed with a sore throat; I joked with Bill about which one of us had found the anagram words first in the paper; I met and sized up Judy's new date; I had a serious talk with Margie about a traffic ticket she had received; and I volunteered to go to the library with young Eddie. Changed the baby once or twice, too. I spent about an hour and a half altogether with the children and many times while I was alone with one of them the others would be right there in the room."

"Do the others try to get in the act when you want to be alone with just one?"

"Not so much any more, Bill. My children realize that their turns will come along. I do try to be fair with them."

January 15

Leonard DeNunzio, 15, had stolen a car. Leonard surprised me with his intelligence: he read every time he could find a quiet spot in the small house crowded with ten children and their parents.

One additional noisy factor was Mr. DeNunzio, who drank steadily from the time he arrived home until he fell into bed at 9 p.m. each night.

"What do you and your father do together, just the two of you, Leonard?" I asked.

It took Leonard some seconds to think of an answer. Then he said,

"He took me to an Italian movie once in '58 or '59, but I don't understand Italian."

Mr. DeNunzio's attitude toward his son seemed to be, "Go it alone."

Back at the picnic ground, my friend Ed continued. "We try to remember that our children are interested in being with other people and in being by themselves. Take young Eddie, for instance. He was reading a book, and when I asked him to come to the picnic today, he said he would rather stay home. So, of course, I let him."

August 15

No matter what Mike's parents asked him to do, he wanted to do something else. Mike was seventeen.

"What did you do last weekend, Mike?" I asked him.

"Same old thing, Mr. George. Everybody piled into the car and went up to the farm to see my grandfather."

"All of you?"

"All of us."

Mike's father was like a drill sergeant with his nine children. When he faced right, all of his children did, too.

I've met fathers who tell me the reason they have so many children is that they love babies.

October 13

"I like my work, Mr. George," the professionally successful man assured me. "And, I love to play with the younger children."

I thought I knew then what his problem was with Tony, 16. Tony had been loved and played with by his father when Tony was young.

Now Tony was too old to like it any longer.

Having six children of our own puts us parents on the treadmill, too. We have cub scouts, girl scouts, pajama parties, school athletic contests, study sessions, movies, carpools, great books programs—and we often feel we are poorly paid partners in the Fresh Air Taxi Cab Company. But, I often think of the older lady who years ago made the comment to me, the comment I've never forgotten, "When you have children you are never alone."

To which I can reply today, "And, what's wrong with that?"

34. THE SMALL FAMILY

Picture a yardstick. At one end is the youngster who is so shy at fifteen he can only answer, "I don't know." Going across the yardstick, we see other young men with some of the specific problems mentioned in this book—underachievement, dropping-out of school, associating with the wrong group of friends. At the far end of the yardstick is the youngster who seems completely selfish in his search for immediate pleasure, sadistic in his dealings with others, violently rebellious against authority. In a paragraph I've tried to give a complete range of behavior, from the youngster who does not compete to the youngster who competes too hard.

November 7   John Simonek, 15, had a definite pattern when asked a question. He would turn to his mother and wait for her to answer.

December 3   I stopped by the house. John, his mother and I sat in the living room. I asked him, "What have you been doing lately, John?"

"Yah, tell him all the trouble you been in," said his mother.

I tried again on a different tack. "How's school going, John?"

"Yah, tell him how miserable your marks are," his mother answered.

"Let's go grab a milk shake, John," I continued, and I thought for a moment Mrs. Simonek was going to put her coat on, too.

John was starving for someone to talk to him, not past him.

You may decide that you know, from your experiences years ago, how your son should be raised today.

May 23	Larry's mother balked at letting him attend a neighborhood party.
	Then she agreed reluctantly to let him go, even if there WERE girls at the party, on the condition that he would be home at 10 p.m.
	Larry knew the party would just be starting to roll at 10 p.m.
	Larry was a senior in high school, about 6' 2", and weighed close to 200 pounds.
April 28	Tears slid down ten-year-old Ralph's cheeks. "I'm the only boy in the whole school that has to wear a suit coat every day."
	The teachers were pleased because Ralph was the best dressed boy in the class. Ralph's father was pleased because the father had worn a suit coat in class years ago, too.
	The difference was that all the boys in the father's class had worn suit coats.

The more children in a family, the more the parents can say to themselves, "We thought he would be successful in ——, but he didn't come up to our expectations. Maybe the next child in line will be successful."

December 12

Larry Ferrantello, 11, came in because he was failing the fifth grade for the second time: yet, a tutor, who had been coming to the house for three years, maintained the young man could do C work.

Mr. Ferrantello spent his weekends in the winter-time driving Larry, an only son, hundreds of miles so the boy could play organized hockey. In the summertime, baseball replaced hockey.

School was important for Mr. Ferrantello because good athletes get scholarships and then become professional baseball or hockey players.

Mr. Ferrantello had been a sandlot baseball player years ago.

December 8

Tom, 18, will graduate from high school next June. He can work during his vacations in his father's business, but if he takes a day off, no one complains. When Tom finishes college he will step into the family business.

Tom was accepted at the university of his choice, but when his

parents chose another school, he
promptly acceded to their wishes.
His comment was, "I'll go to the
school my parents want me to.
Then, if I flunk out, I can blame
them."

Time will tell whether Tom will
ever make his own decisions.

If you must place all your dreams in one balloon,
prepare for the balloon to explode one day.

Parents in small families have a tendency to become
child-oriented, that is, to make every decision, whether
the child is concerned or not, considered or not, considered in the light of "What will Johnny think of this
action?"

March 8	When the alarm clock rang at the McIntosh home, everybody went into action. Father, mother, and both grandparents had an immediate objective—to get Chipper out of bed. Chipper stayed in bed enjoying the commotion he was causing.
September 17	Bobby, 12, was one of the most self-centered young men I've met. He liked school, he said, but not the teachers. Bobby's father agreed with his son; if Bobby was kept after

school for misbehavior, the father would go to work on the teacher.

If Bobby fought with a schoolmate, his father was ready to take on the schoolmate's father.

Anything Bobby wanted to do, in effect, was fine with his father.

Bobby's future doesn't need a crystal ball...he will become more selfish. On the day he commits his first major crime, his father will be there with the best lawyer in town.

October 18

The grandmother was shrewd. Jim, 13, was only able to get by her one time before she realized he was using her to write phony excuses to get him out of class.

Jim's mother agreed to stop writing phony excuses for her son.

May 17

Jim's school counselor surprised me in documenting eight different occasions when his mother had signed phony notes to excuse him from school.

What did Jim's mother want, what was best for Jim, or what Jim, at thirteen, wanted?

A few chapters ago, we discussed "Violence." Transfer of anger, there covered in some detail, can easily focus on the child in a small family; if you and your wife have unpleasant words when you arrive from work, who is it that gets sent to bed without his supper?

Two extremes, then, are often found in the only child. The child may be a shy, fearful, dependent person, or be willful, aggressive, and self-seeking. To prevent either of these unpleasant developments in your family, I suggest research and development. By "research" I mean *your* research: like a man who would read only last year's sport pages and consequently not know who won this year's Masters' golf tournament at Augusta, the father of a small family can also fall asleep by failing to investigate how fathers of neighboring families have acted in specific situation. By "development" I mean your *son's* development: the young man has to learn the give-and-take of social situations outside your home. He needs, more than members of a larger family, to associate with other children, so he will learn NOT to be willful, aggressive, and self-seeking.

Don't be too discouraged please. You have one big advantage over those fathers with larger families. While I have to remember to split my time equally among my six, whatever time you spend individually with your fine son is all his.

35. MASTURBATION

By "masturbation" I mean your son's "obtaining sexual satisfaction by manual stimulation of his genitals." When your son was physically developed enough so that he could masturbate, he may have formed the habit before he realized there are sexual overtones to masturbation; after he realized there was something sexual about masturbation, the habit might have become difficult to break. Your son may want help breaking the habit and yet find a discussion with you quite difficult.

So, I suggest you ask your son to read this chapter with this thought in your minds—if he casually mentions to you in the next week or so that he would like an appointment with your family clergyman or doctor your son may be signalling that he would like to know more about masturbation.

If your son asks for an appointment, please arrange one at your early convenience, *without* discussing masturbation with your son yourself before or after his appointment.

If your son tells you, "Dad, I'd like to talk to you some night about something I read in *Understanding Your Teenage Boy*" you can reply, "Sure, son. Give me about a week to do a little reasearch and we'll have a talk," and then read a current discussion about masturbation yourself. (Our bibliography, on page 159, contains several excellent sources of information.)

Before becoming unduly alarmed yourself, Dad, realize that many young men your son's age are concerned with masturbation and would like some kindly information on the subject.

36. DEATH OF A BROTHER OR SISTER

My beloved father wasn't feeling well. He had had a series of minor heart attacks, as many as eight in a single day, and medication was having no effect. To cheer him, I told him the story of the old man in the oxygen tent who called his son to the bedside and said, "Son, I've been pretty good to you throughout your life. I paid for your education started you in business, bought you your Cadillacs. There's one favor I'd like to ask of you."

"Anything," the son replied. "What is it?"

"Get your foot off that oxygen tube."

Not three weeks later my father was in an oxygen tent himself; we kept the watch as his pulse became more feeble. Suddenly he signalled us to come close to the ten, and, with a feeble chuckle, said, "Get YOUR foot off that oxygen tube."

I've seen timely death: I've seen untimely death, too.

The sudden death of a child is certainly untimely. Few events are more catastrophic to a family than having a youngster at the dinner table one night and at the funeral parlor the next. Etched in the minds of parents and the living children are the last experiences with the now dead youngster.

Competing with a dead angel is murder for the living adolescent; unless your living son was into his late teens when the death occurred, he had the usual and natural rivalries with the now dead child. Like the teen-ager I know who felt *he* was the reason why his father had had a heart attack and died (after a game of catch), your son may feel unnecessarily guilty. And, your son may be relieved when his competitor dies, and feel guilty in his relief. After all, a rival for something your living son values highly, individual companionship with you, has now been removed from the picture.

Grant, then, the possibilities of remorse and guilt being naturally present in your living child when a brother or sister dies suddenly. These feelings can be intensified when parents compare living children with the now dead child.

October 11	Tom Osborn, 17, had forged his mother's name to $265 worth of bad checks.
	To say that Mrs. Osborn was upset was an understatement. I kept thinking she would reach into her pocketbook for an itemized list of Tom's faults over the years, but no, she had them memorized.
	She dwelt on the slow death of Linda, then 10, five years ago, and became tearful in the memory.
October 28	Tom started to straighten out but Mrs. Osborn could see no improvement. She commented several times, "If only Linda hadn't died," as if the family problems would not have existed if only Linda were still alive.
	Linda, his mother would tell Tom, would not have gotten into "this" trouble, whatever trouble

Tom was currently in. Linda would have been perfect.

All of Mrs. Osborn's hopes had jumped from the living to the what-might-have-been.

It is difficult for a parent not to wrap his ambitions in the dead child, not to say to himself, "Life would have been so much better if only my child had not died." But, would it? Perhaps the good God took your child out of this life before he encountered trouble.

A living son cannot forget his guilt and remorse as long as his parents make indirect comparisons.

March 29   Harold Rice, 15, came in because he had "high intelligence" and low marks.

April-June   We ascertained that Harold had an average intelligence, and when his parents stopped grounding him for D's, his marks improved to C's.

The sudden death of older brother Mark last year kept being mentioned.

Mr. Rice, for a five month period of mourning, had only been sober during duty hours at the telephone company. Other times he would quietly, competently, drink himself to sleep.

The thought must have crossed Harold's mind, "If I were to die,

would Dad drink or feel relieved?"

Much better, I believe is the following attitude toward a child who died an untimely death.

April   "Mary Kay," I said to a lady I respect, "I was thinking the other
day about the first time we met.
You were living on Marlowe, and
I brought over a present to you
from Rosemary. You were in bed
trying to carry a baby full term.
Do you remember?"

"Surely. Rosemary sent me a
prayer book."

"Were you pregnant with Diane
then?"

"No," she answered. "With
Jimmy, the one who died."

Period.

5

Situations Not Discussed Specifically

37. THE LAST WORD

Once more I ask you to assume that you and I are friends; you stop by my office one noon hour and ask me to go out to lunch. I agree, and then I say, "I forgot. Today's my day to play squash. How about coming along with me for about forty-five minutes of fast exercise?"

"No thanks," you reply. "I haven't taken any violent exercise for years. Might have a heart attack."

"We won't exercise enough to hurt you. Come on along."

"I never played the game," you protest.

"Played tennis?"

"A few times as a kid. I had all the shots but I never was good enough to play in tournaments."

Finally, reluctantly, you agree to go to the squash court with me.

You enter a squash court through a small door which fits flush with the back wall when you close the door. You are in a brightly lighted room about the size of a $2\frac{1}{2}$ car garage; the walls are about twice as high as the standard living room walls. Your racket is longer than a tennis racket and has a smaller head; the ball is black, hard rubber, and about the size of a golf ball. Each player must hit his shot in rotation to the front wall before the ball bounces twice on the floor or his opponent wins a point. It is not unusual for the ball to bounce off the front wall, side wall, and then the back wall. A fast game.

No matter how much tennis you have played, I'll guarantee you one thing—the first time you play squash with me you will be terrible. You will be awkward, inept, uncoordinated.

How should I treat you if I want you to continue to play squash with me?

Would you be encouraged to play squash with me if I ridiculed your efforts to hit the ball?

June 1   The father and the son sat as far away from each other as they could.

The father said, "I've been telling that little stinker to shape up or ship out."

The little stinker was thirteen.

Would you be inclined to practice squash if I held the door open for you, ushered you inside, and said, "Go ahead. Get some practice."

March 7   "My dad? He's ok, but he works all the time."

November 2   "My dad is a man who pushes buttons all day long."

January 9   The little boy had a surprising amount of anger bubbling just below the surface.

Nice, hard-working parents were always home at the proper times.

Maybe he touched on the problem when he told me about asking his mother to play cribbage with him one night. With the iron in her hand, she replied, "Go wash your face and get ready for bed."

I asked him, "How much ironing does your mother do?"

"Every night."

No time for cribbage.

Suppose I told you three times that you would get more power into a backhand drive by having your right foot extended and then you still hit the next ball girlishly, off your left foot. Should I blow my stack?

May 27

"My son knows that he is to close the backyard gate after I back the car out in the morning. Yesterday he tried to close the gate WHILE I was backing the new car out."

"What did you do?" I asked.

"I beat him to within an inch of his life," the father said, exultantly.

Do I have to watch every shot you make, or should I get myself into position to return your shots?

June 17

"Let him go out? Not on your life. That brat of mine would only get himself into trouble."

May 2   "I can't trust that kid out of my
                   sight."

How would you feel if you and I stepped inside the
court to play, and I said, "Oh, I forgot. Today I'm
playing with Ed Jackson. You stand over in the corner
and watch us. You'll pick up a lot that way"?

February 19   The Montgomerys enjoyed their
                   before-dinner cocktails together.
                   While the parents drank and
                   talked in the family room, the chil-
                   dren ate in the kitchen.

October 10   The Edisons had enough money to
                   buy a summer home which was
                   more like a mansion. The four
                   children spent summers there with
                   a nurse and a caretaker.
                       The parents often would visit
                   the cottage weekends.

Teaching you to play squash wouldn't be too difficult. Knowing that you had never played before, I
wouldn't expect much progress at the beginning. We'd
laugh at your clumsiness but you would know that I enjoy your companionship. I would praise you every time
you hit the ball to the front wall, even though you hit
it there only once in your first ten attempts. I would
try to demonstrate how to hit each shot, even those
tough ones which ricochet off the side wall, before you
would face the shot in competition. I would not tell

you how uncoordinated you are in comparison with more talented players I know. If you were to ask me how to play a difficult shot, I would listen to see that I understood your question and then demonstrate how to react. I would spend a lot of time alone with you in the courts. We'd have a lot of laughs.

And, when you got as good as I, and wanted to play with someone else, I'd say, "Go ahead. Enjoy yourself."

6
Suggested Reading

Rather than direct you to some of the more technical texts used in writing this book, I have searched out several books along the same lines, books which are clearly written for the layman, books which I think you will enjoy.

Leo J. Trese's *Parent and Child* (New York: Sheed and Ward, 1962; paperback edition: St. Meinrad, Ind.: ABBEY PRESS, Fall, 1968) should be kept on the shelf next to your bed. His chapter on the difference between discipline and punishment is superb; Fr. Trese likes children and parents.

W. W. Bauer's book, *Moving into Manhood* (New York: Doubleday, 1963), has two excellent chapters, "You're Almost a Man," and "Girls Are Growing Up, Too."

For a clear discussion of sex, you might pick up *Your Child and Sex* (New York: Random House, 1964), by another Catholic priest, George A. Kelly. He discusses eleven principles of sex education and his "How to Tell your Child About Sex" chapters are worth your time.

Training the Adolescent (Milwaukee: Bruce, 1937), by R. C. McCarthy, has some interesting information in his chapters on "Mental Growth and Reconstruction" and "Physical Development of the Adolescent."

MARRIAGE PAPERBACKS

Popularly priced, authoritative books on Marriage and Family Life

FAMILY HANDBOOK OF DOLLARS AND SENSE By William Whalen
20001 .... 50¢

HELP YOUR CHILD ENJOY BOOKS By Margery Frisbie
20002 .... 50¢

A DO-IT-YOURSELF GUIDE TO HOLY HOUSEWIFERY Ethel Marbach
20003 .... 75¢

FAMILY FUN AND RECREATION By Richard Frisbie
20004 .... 50¢

SEX IN YOUR MARRIAGE Foreword by Blaise Hettich, O.S.B.
20005 .... 75¢

KEEP YOUR FAMILY HEALTHY By Charles Gerras
20007 .... 50¢

MARRIED LOVE Foreword by C. Q. Mattingly
20008 .... 75¢

HUSBAND AND FATHER By John H. Ford
20011 .... 50¢

ARE THESE THE WONDERFUL YEARS? A family life omnibus
20012 .... 50¢

WE TRIED THIS Practical solutions to everyday family problems
20013 .... 50¢

WHAT TO DO BEFORE JOHNNY GOES TO SCHOOL Paul Herbert
20014 .... 50¢

MIXED MARRIAGE: An Honest Appraisal
20016 .... 75¢

GETTING READY FOR YOUR WEDDING By Charles & Rita Strubbe
20017 .... 75¢

A WOMAN'S WAY By Mary Lewis Coakley
20018 .... 75¢

AN ADVENTURE IN LOVE By Franz Weyergans
20019 .... 75¢

DIARY OF A NEW MOTHER By Jeanne Davis Glynn
20020 .... 75¢

I HAVE THIS PERFECTLY MARVELOUS WOMAN WHO COMES IN
BY THE DAY AND IT'S ME By Juneil Parmenter
20022 .... 75¢

ART, OBSCENITY AND YOUR CHILDREN By Clayton C. Barbeau
20023 .... 95¢

WHERE TO GET HELP FOR YOUR FAMILY By Anne M. Tansey
20024 .... 75¢

SEX AND PERSONAL GROWTH By Reginald Trevett
20025 .... 95¢

THE DO-IT-YOURSELF PARENT By Richard & Margery Frisbie
20026 .... 95¢

THE QUIET POSSIBLE SHE By Janet Golden
20028 .... 95¢

ABBEY PRESS, ST. MEINRAD, INDIANA 47577